THE

SENTIMENTAL PERSON'S

GUIDE
TO

decluttering

Claire Middleton

Author of *Downsizing Your Life for Freedom, Flexibility and Financial Peace*

PARKER-ELGIN PRESS

Published by: Parker-Elgin Press, an imprint of Cardamom Publishers
P.O. Box 743, Janesville, WI 53547

Library of Congress Control Number: 2018964669
Library of Congress Subject Heading: Housekeeping, Housecleaning

ISBN 978-0-9980453-0-6

BISAC: House & Home/Cleaning, Caretaking & Organizing,
Code HOM019000

Table of Contents

TABLE OF CONTENTS

For everything there is a season, and a time for every matter under heaven...a time to keep, and a time to cast away.

Ecclesiastes 3:1,6b

Introduction

When you feel claustrophobic in your own home, or you give up cleaning because there's just too much stuff to clean around, it's time to declutter.

When you get to the point where there are things you'd like to do with your living space, but you can't because there's no room, it's time to declutter.

When you know there's a move in your future, and those old boxes full of stuff you haven't opened in ages will drive up the cost of that move, it's time to declutter.

So why *don't* you declutter?

Many of us fail to declutter, no matter how motivated we are to do so, because of the many obstacles to decluttering, a simple process that (in theory) shouldn't be very hard.

And one of the biggest obstacles to decluttering is being sentimental.

The challenge of decluttering when you're a sentimental person is that you may be so nostalgic that *everything* has sentimental value to you:

Oh, wow! I just found all the sheet music from my childhood piano lessons! (Your fingers haven't touched piano keys in ten years.)

Oh, look! It's the cap off the beer my dad was drinking when our team won the World Series! (That bottle cap should have been pitched long ago.)

Oh, my! It's my hotel soap bar collection! (The traveling sales rep job ended years ago.)

Sentimental people see the memory value in everything. We're so sensitive that even the most mediocre, unassuming item can have special meaning to us. Family and friends look at us like we're nuts: they're thinking, "Who else but *you* would have kept that?"

There's nothing wrong with being sentimental. Personally, I suspect people who have zero memories attached to anything, who become so minimalist that their life goal is to keep only a cup, a plate and a blanket, are actually pretty cold-blooded.

But we sentimentalists get into trouble when we keep so many things for sentimental reasons that our collection of possessions begins to overwhelm us. And when we try to cut back, to declutter, to reduce our burden, we quickly get stuck and want to give up because it's just too hard to let go of so many things that have sentimental meaning to us.

I wrote this book to help those who want to live with less stuff, to feel that freedom of being unburdened by full attics and packed basements, but who have trouble because they're sentimental people. I relate to you, because I've been there.

I kept far too many items from my youth and from the many years we spent raising our large family. As a result, we ended up with a basement packed full of stuff. How I would dream of the whole basement flooding so we'd have to pitch everything, or later on, that the storage units we rented would burn down so I wouldn't have to deal with all the decisions we had to make about what to keep and what to give away or throw out. I knew that most of our accumulation could go, but there was a nucleus of important papers, photos that never made it into albums, paper memorabilia of our immediate family's history, and small keepsake items that I wanted to save. Knowing I had to find that nucleus is what kept me chipping away at it instead of praying for a monsoon or becoming an arsonist.

But I didn't start chipping away at it until I was forced to: a financial setback in 2007 required us to sell the big house where we raised our family for nearly 20 years and move to much smaller quarters. That meant we had to get rid of more than half of our possessions. Most of the stuff was items I kept because they had sentimental value to me. They were so hard to give up, because it felt like I wasn't just letting go of items, but of memories and happy feelings as well.

But that experience taught me that giving up belongings I thought I could never let go of was worth the time it took and the emotional pain I felt, because we now live with far fewer possessions very happily and comfortably.

I no longer feel the stress of...

... walking through stacks of boxes of stuff in the basement just to get to the washing machine,

... paying good money for storage units full of stuff we never use in our daily lives, or

... feeling the mental weight of knowing there are closets packed tight that I need to go through.

I'm free of all that, and it feels so good!

Many sentimental people never get to experience that freedom: keeping possessions long after they don't need them because they're emotionally attached to them leads to large amounts of clutter packed everywhere, causing feelings of lethargy and even despair. Perhaps that's where you're at right now.

Take heart; you *can* change your situation, with the help of the stories and tips you'll find in this book.

So...

...if you want to live with more space and less clutter,

...if you want to make your home seem larger and your family feel more comfortable thanks to more open space,

...if you want the room to try new things, whether it's floor space so you can practice yoga, or attic space so you can set up an art studio...

...this book will help you reach that feeling of lightness and freedom without regret.

You'll discover:

- strategies for giving up many of your sentimental items,

- what you can learn from people who aren't sentimental,

- three rules for decluttering success (for sentimental people only!),
- and the four steps of the decluttering process.

You'll also learn how to sort and categorize your sentimental items, with specifics for the seven groups of items that are the hardest to give up: what I call the Sentimental Seven.

Finally, we'll take a brief look at how to encourage those you live with to go through their own sentimental clutter.

There's nothing wrong with being a sentimental person. In fact, we sentimental types tend to be very kind, caring people. But our sentimental nature can become a burden to us when it comes to our possessions. You wouldn't have chosen this book if you weren't feeling overwhelmed by the sum total of what you've kept for sentimental reasons.

I hope this book will help you greatly *reduce* the number of sentimental belongings you own, but not eliminate them entirely, because that's not the goal. As sentimental people, we *need* to keep some tangible items that warm our hearts. That's how we're wired. And we need to be able to see them regularly. We'll discuss some ideas for doing that in this book.

Ultimately, this will be a challenging and rewarding exercise. It will tax your emotions and your energy, it will take time, and you'll have to keep reassuring yourself that you're not a failure if you don't get rid of *all* your sentimental clutter.

But in the end, when you see more open space in your house, when you can open a closet without flinching, when you can walk through a room and admire a couple of treasures (while not tripping over anything), you'll feel a sense of lightness and freedom that will make you wish you had done this much sooner.

So let's get started!

Chapter 1

Decluttering: The Sentimental Person's Challenge

We live in an age of stuff. People buy stuff all the time, in stores and online. People give gifts to each other for every possible occasion, thus adding to others' piles of stuff. Soon people find that their homes are overstuffed with stuff and they have to rent storage units where they can keep old stuff so they can make room in their homes for more new stuff.

Some people will always live like this. Someday they'll die and their kids or other relatives will have to go through it all, and they'll curse them even as they mourn their passing, because they left them with such an enormous burden.

Others, like you and me, will either be forced to deal with our own stuff or will become sick of all the clutter in our homes. But in the past, whenever we tried to go through it, we failed because we put almost everything into the "Keep" bag.

(In this book, we'll use the decluttering method where you go through your home, room by room, and put things into one of three bags: Keep, Donate, or Trash. Some people add a fourth bag marked Sell, because, thanks to garage sales and eBay, there are ways to make some money off of your clutter.)

This sorting-into-bags method works just fine for some people. But for sentimental people, it doesn't work as well because we put nothing but actual garbage in the Trash bag, we put only a few items in the Donate and Sell bags, and we have to go find more bags for what we want to keep, because we've already filled a half-dozen bags marked Keep.

Is there no hope for the sentimental person? Are we doomed to live in clutter because we love too many things too much?

No! We too can enjoy clutter-free homes. I will show you how to feel much better about giving away some of your belongings, maybe even *most* of your belongings, with little regret.

Note that I didn't say ALL of your belongings. Some people are minimalists and can live on "a loaf of bread, a jug of wine and Thou." I admire those people but I'm not one of them. Sentimental people have a very hard time being minimalists, because we need a cushion of our most precious things to get through life. That's just how we're wired, and there's nothing wrong with that. But a problem develops when we don't reign ourselves in: we end up being suffocated by too many things that we love, cherish or see as having incredible historic or monetary value.

Sentimental people are loving, giving people who treasure their memories. (Did you know that most pack-rats are sentimental types?) But we sometimes find that we actually hate our precious things even though we love them, because they're weighing us down and making us feel stifled and even overwhelmed.

You wouldn't be interested in decluttering unless the sheer quantity of your stuff was becoming a burden for you. But unlike those unsentimental types who have no trouble decluttering, you need to consider your nature as you go through the process. By winnowing down to your most precious items, you can keep what means most to you while getting rid of all the burdensome stuff. Then you can live an uncluttered life while being able to see and enjoy the things you love most, things that remind you of people you love, times you loved and places you loved.

So if you feel suffocated by too many belongings that you love and can't give up, take heart: there *is* a way out.

What Do People Get Sentimental About?

Hotel soap bars, sheet music and beer bottle caps are just a few examples of mundane items that we sentimental people become attached to and refuse to give up. But most of the time, it's not the items themselves that are valuable, but what they represent or remind us of that's important to us. The things we have the hardest time giving up include:

- Things that belonged to a late loved one
- Things that belonged to our kids
- Things that reflect our past accomplishments

- Things that remind us of happier times

- Things that remind us of the people we used to be and the things we used to do

- Things that represent our unfulfilled plans and dreams

- Things that were given to us by someone we love(d)

While most of our stuff isn't all that valuable in a financial sense, whoever or whatever it reminds us of is very precious to us. That's why it's so hard to give it up. And indeed, the goal is not to give it *all* up. But when you have way too much, your overload of belongings becomes an albatross around your neck. So the trick is to get rid of *enough* of your sentimental clutter while keeping only the most precious items; that way, you'll finally have enough space to keep those most precious items where you can access and enjoy them.

You may also have some items that you feel that you "should" keep, even though you personally may not be that crazy about them. Perhaps you inherited a set of china that isn't your style, but your late aunt left them to you and it would break her heart if you got rid of them. So they take up space in your attic (and your mind). Your desire to give them up conflicts with your guilt over doing just that, so you decide not to decide, and leave those boxes where they've been sitting for years, hogging space you could really use for something else. Postponing such decisions is why your past decluttering efforts failed; instead of getting rid of things, you just rearranged the clutter into neater, tighter piles, because you couldn't deal with all the tough decisions.

You chose to continue storing sentimental things, but what good is that? You can't see those items, so they can't remind you of the reason you kept them (a person, an event or a time period.) If something is that special to you, it should be on display or at least accessible. And you only have so much space, so you can't keep all of it. That's why you need to decide what to keep and what to let go of; you simply don't have room for all of it.

For sentimental people, the most difficult part of decluttering is the decision-making that comes with it. If we cared only for the monetary value of our belongings, we could just winnow out whatever isn't worth much money. But by definition, a sentimental person cares more about the feelings generated by their things than the cash those things might generate.

In this book, you'll learn how to make those tough decisions. You'll also see that *where* you send your sentimental items is very important. Instead of pitching belongings you kept for sentimental reasons, which can be very painful, you can choose to give things to people who need them or can be helped by them. This eases the pain of letting go, so you'll feel better.

You'll be reminded that your sentimental clutter can't help anyone if it's buried away; in fact, it's sitting there, breaking down and decomposing, in your closet, basement, attic or storage unit(s) right at this moment. Letting it go so it can help someone is a great way to honor the memory it represents, especially if it once belonged to someone you lost.

You'll also learn how to determine which of your many sentimental items have the most significance to *you*, not to your late Aunt Minnie, or your cousins who expect you to be the keeper of the flame for the family by storing heirlooms for which *they* have no room in *their* homes.

You'll find out how to let go of many items from when you were a child, and when your children were children. You'll also learn what to do with old gifts as well as collections that you've kept for far too many years.

By using specific strategies for giving up items that have sentimental value to you, you can face the challenge of decluttering while dealing with those items in a meaningful way. That really does make the process a lot easier. It also helps with regret, which is a major challenge for sentimental people. We can admit that we'd be willing to let go of certain things except that we're afraid we'll regret doing so later on. That was one of my major fears before I was forced to give up so many memory-laden items when we downsized. Fortunately, the strategies in this book minimize regret very well; in fact, I can't remember most of what I got rid of back then. I do have photos of them, but I never look at them. I don't feel the need to do so anymore. I've found that by letting go of the past, I can enjoy the present much more.

As you work your way through this book, you'll figure out why you've kept what you've kept, and whether or not it's still important to you (important enough to keep, and to take up valuable space in your home). This is the goal: keep only what is still meaningful to you, and put it where you can see it and appreciate it.

The Advantage to Being a 21st Century Declutterer

For many of us, the hardest part about giving up items we're emotionally attached to is that we're afraid if we give up the item, we'll lose the memory. I know that's a possibility because the memory of something I haven't thought about in years often only comes back to me when I see an item related to the memory that triggers it. So it does seem like giving up our sentimental items could mean losing the good memories they bring back, too. But there's a simple solution to this problem.

In this book, I frequently recommend an inexpensive technique that we're fortunate to have available to us as 21st century declutterers. It lets us keep the memories that our sentimental items trigger without keeping all the items themselves. This technique is digital photography.

By taking photos of anything we're emotionally attached to that we must get rid of, we can continue to enjoy our sentimental items. If you fear that just seeing a photo of something you gave up will only make you regret doing so, you can store away the photos in the cloud, on a memory card (such as those sold by SanDisk and other manufacturers), a thumb drive or a file in your computer. That way, you know the photos are there if you want to see them, but you won't be accidentally reminded of what you gave up, because it will take some effort to find them.

As for those of us who *love* seeing reminders of our past, these photos can be made into screensavers for our computers, slide shows for our digital picture frames or even scrapbooks that we can read and enjoy whenever we wish. (Websites like **shutterfly.com** or **snapfish.com** make it easy to turn digital photos into professional-looking scrapbooks.)

Suppose you have a dozen dolls from childhood that you just can't keep anymore. You can ask someone to take photos of you holding each doll. Write up a story about how you got each doll, what their names are, where you lived when you got them, how you played with them, etc. Then include each story on a page with the appropriate photo, and turn the pages into a digital scrapbook. This way you can keep all those memories and see your dolls without letting them take up a lot of space. Someday your scrapbook will be a treasure for your children, grandchildren and other loved ones to enjoy. If it's too hard to give up all your dolls, you could keep your very favorite, and you'd still have all the others in your scrapbook to look at whenever you wish.

Keep in mind that in a photo, a treasured item continues to look good. In reality, had you kept the physical item, it would fade, dry out, get moldy or deteriorate in some other way over time. The photo actually preserves the item, in a way.

Digital photography is also a great way to save family history in the form of letters, genealogies and old photos. Scan them and save them to your computer: you can even create a book of family history and give copies to your relatives.

This method also works for collectors who need to reduce or give up a collection. It could be done with:

- Record album covers

- T-shirt collections

- Figurines and other collectibles

- Sports cards

- Souvenirs from your travels

...to name just a few. And it's an especially good way to deal with large, cumbersome items like ornate vintage oil lamps (I know someone who has dozens of these on rows of shelves that require constant dusting) or small, fragile items like glass stemware (for instance, one woman's collection of antique Italian bud vases).

Throughout this book, you'll see references to taking photos of the items you still like but are giving up. It's a great option that requires only the simple step of taking a photo with your phone or camera.

Don't Be Afraid

I used to hate the thought of opening up a box I hadn't opened in years with the goal of getting rid of its contents. I was afraid I'd have a big emotional struggle with myself before closing the box back up and deciding to face it some other time (that's the Scarlett O'Hara method: "Tomorrow is another day!") My fear perpetuated a cycle of decluttering procrastination that continued for years until we were finally forced to deal with our clutter.

You may also fear tackling your sentimental clutter, thinking it will be too difficult to part with a single thing, as it always has been before. That fear of failing again may be fighting your desire to have an uncluttered home.

But it's important to realize that we all change as we age, so it's likely that some of the things you once adored will no longer look so good to you. You may even wonder why you kept them! That's why I recommend going through everything once and giving up anything that no longer interests you, or seems worth keeping. The momentum you gain from doing so will give you confidence, which will help you when you have to make tougher decisions about the rest.

Keep What You Will Use...And Use It!

Remember, you don't have to get rid of *everything*. If you have useful items stored away that you truly believe you'll use, keep them, but put them to use right away. For instance, Jenny just couldn't give up her late mom's good china, but she didn't have room to store it, either. So she donated her own dinnerware to Goodwill; now her family uses "Grandma's china" every day. Yes, some plates have been chipped. But at least the set isn't sitting untouched in the attic anymore. Jenny feels close to her mom every time she uses one of the dishes.

Andrea likes to wear an apron when she cooks, so she kept two of her grandmother's aprons and uses them all the time. Linda uses linen handkerchiefs, including some from her late aunt. And Dorrie loves the compliments she gets on the hip vintage jewelry she wears, most of which was her great aunt's.

When my eldest was young, I gave her a couple of my very favorite stuffed animals that I had saved from my childhood. She played with them for quite a while, and gave them lots of love. Even though I thought I would never give them up, after picking them up off the floor with her other toys day after day, they eventually lost their "specialness" to me. I don't remember what happened to them, but I do know that letting her play with them made a lot more sense than leaving them in a box in storage. Using an item you're sentimentally attached to shows a lot more love and respect for it than letting it molder away in an attic or a basement. But if you can't use it, why not pass it along so someone else can give it that love and respect?

The decluttering process is the key to taking control of our homes and the possessions in them so that we can create the kind of home we truly desire. This means removing items that are no longer needed or truly loved so that we can enjoy more open space and also make room for the occasional new decorative item or piece of furniture. Doing this will help us make a comfortable home that reflects our personality.

Ultimately, if you keep more items than you can use, you will come to see the excess as a burden (if you don't already!)

Becoming a Sentimental Declutterer

I know "Sentimental Declutterer" sounds like an oxymoron, but it's not. Your sentimental nature is part of your personality, but that doesn't mean it has to control your behavior. If you have a desire for a clean, uncluttered-looking home, you can have it, but it will take self-discipline, common sense and realistic thinking.

By using the techniques and thought processes in this book, you can clean up your act despite your sentimental nature.

That said, many of us are a little too proud of being sentimental; when others give us a hard time about how many belongings we've chosen to keep, we look at them as lacking in sentimental feelings. In fact, I used to think that people who aren't sentimental are kind of cold, sometimes even heartless. And some of them are, especially when it comes to clearing out others' belongings. But they don't usually live amidst a houseful of clutter, and many of them have an important personal characteristic that some of us sentimental types lack, as we'll see in the next chapter.

———◆◉◆———

Chapter 1 in a Nutshell:

Decluttering is much harder for the sentimental person, but it can be done, with the right techniques and encouragement.

Chapter 2

The Opposite of Sentimental: Clean-Sweepers

My mother is one of those people who can easily throw things away, especially things that don't belong to her. I, on the other hand, am very sentimental, and as a child I loved every single one of my dolls, toys and games.

Mom learned early on that I wasn't going to give up my belongings easily, so she tried shaming me: "See how nice and clean your sister's side of the room is? But yours is a mess! She only has one little statue on her side of the dresser, but your side is covered!"

Yes, my side was covered, with treasures I had amassed from visits to amusement parks, books I bought with my allowance, trinkets I had gotten out of candy machines—everything I owned carried a good memory with it. While my sister's twin bed was decorated with one perfectly coiffed bride doll propped on her pillow, my much-loved and thus wild-haired bride doll shared my pillow with my bean bag puppy, my Bozo doll (cherished since infancy) and several other beloved creatures, all of whom showed the wear of my affections. We won't even get into my Barbie and Ken doll collection, which was packed into my side of the closet.

The clutter resulting from my tendency to be attached to *all* my belongings drove Mom crazy, so she came up with another plan. Once in a while, something of mine would just disappear. After school, I'd walk into my bedroom and notice that my side of the dresser seemed a little empty, like a few items were missing. If I knew exactly what was missing, I'd ask my mother and she'd feign ignorance.

Her little successes emboldened her. As more children were born to our family, Mom got worse, to the point that it finally became common knowledge that Mom threw out our stuff regularly while we were at school. Over the years, I learned to hide my most beloved items and to howl with anger whenever something I really loved was missing.

Once I was on my own, I quickly amassed a lot of stuff with no Mom around to perform regular purges. I married another sentimental person, and between the two of us we managed to amply fill a three-bedroom house before we'd had any children.

Then the children began arriving, and the clutter overload multiplied. I was so busy with our children and, later on, our at-home businesses that my occasional decluttering efforts were never completed. It didn't help that I was as attached to many of my children's belongings as they were. Also, in an attempt to be fairer with them than my mother had been with me, I would go through their toys *with* them, letting them keep whatever they loved and getting rid of anything they clearly didn't care about anymore. Wow, was *that* time consuming! But I came through it with a clear conscience (and an overstuffed basement).

A few years after our children began striking out on their own, the economy went south and the business that brought in the lion's share of our family income went with it. You can read the long version of that saga in my book *Downsizing Your Life for Freedom, Flexibility and Financial Peace*; the short version is that we had to empty our large family home of nearly 20 years in three weeks. There was no time to declutter; the necessities were moved to our new rental home four hours away, and the rest was divided between two large storage units in two different towns. Over the next four years, we moved three times, shedding stuff the entire time, until we bought the little house we live in now, having given up more than half of our belongings and emptying both storage units in the process.

So I understand the struggle a sentimental person has when forced to give up beloved possessions. What I don't understand are people like my mother, who have no trouble throwing away large quantities of other people's belongings, including their treasures, without a single thought. (This is the woman who gave our family's collection of home movies to a cousin in another state because they were cluttering up her front hall closet.)

People like my mother think decluttering is just a matter of getting some trash bags, going around the room throwing almost everything in them, and then putting them at the curb. And she's not alone. Consider Kevin, the son of Sandy, who I wrote about in *Downsizing*. After Sandy had a stroke at age 63 and had to move to a nursing home, Kevin took a few items from her house that he wanted, then hired an auctioneer to come in and sell off everything else in it, including the family Bible. Sandy was crushed when she learned about the auction, and mourned the loss of her belongings for a long time. Recently she passed away; I think she died of a broken heart.

I just don't understand people like my mother and Kevin, and I'm betting you don't either. No, we sentimental types don't understand purges of precious things, or throwing nice belongings in dumpsters. Our belongings mean something to us, so it takes quite an effort to give them up.

But sometimes we must. As I learned several years ago, sometimes you're forced to reduce your possessions, no matter how painful doing so might be. And not only can you do it, but you can come through it feeling amazingly light and free. Seriously!

Once we pared down to having just enough belongings to fit comfortably (not snugly) in our little house, I felt freer than I had in many years. I had only my most beloved possessions around me, out where I could see them, plus several plastic boxes in my basement where I can go to relive my memories of my children when they were small.

Everything else is long gone. I don't even remember much of it anymore. And what I do remember, I remember fondly but with little if any regret, because I love living without all the clutter now.

Have They No Heart?

I call people like my mother and Kevin clean-sweepers, because they're so willing to sweep away things that mean a lot to others. It makes me wonder if they have no heart.

And while they may keep a few special somethings for themselves, often it's not much. Among the possessions that Kevin left for the auctioneer to sell were his childhood school photos, his high school graduation photo and other mementos from his youth. As for my mother, some years back she returned to each of my siblings and me our own baby and childhood photos as well as our kids' baby and childhood photos, saying they took up too much space. If it weren't for a group shot of her kids on her bedroom wall, you'd never know she had any!

I don't understand that. My walls are covered with photos of my kids at different ages: group shots and individual shots. And now that I have grandchildren arriving, more photos are popping up around our little house. What a delight!

But even though clean-sweepers like Kevin and my mother mystify me, if I'm honest I have to admit that I envy them a little. For one thing, their homes are open and airy, and they never have to move stacks of plastic or cardboard boxes to get to anything.

They also don't have the mental weight of clutter on their minds all the time. While I now live with much less stuff than I once did, I still have to remain vigilant about what I let into the house. I try to stick to the policy of getting rid of one item every time I bring home something new. But sometimes I fall behind, and when I start seeing little piles around the house, the guilt begins creeping back into my brain. I hate that feeling! I lived with clutter guilt for too many years, and I don't want it back. But it's a constant struggle to stay on top of the clutter battle.

Maybe Clean-Sweepers Aren't Heartless After All

There's one more thing that I envy about clean-sweepers: they care so little about things that they can be very generous to others. Take my old neighbor Caren, for example. Caren was a teacher, married with children, who kept an immaculate home. No, she didn't do the actual cleaning. There was a cleaning lady for that. But Caren didn't let things sit around her house, and this was particularly true of her children's outgrown clothing. In fact, I swear those little dresses her daughter outgrew were still warm when Caren gave them to another neighbor with daughters just a little younger than hers.

And those dresses were absolutely beautiful because Caren liked very nice things; they were designer dresses from stores like Lord and Taylor, and Nordstrom. She could have made good money selling her daughter's old duds online or through a consignment store. But Caren already made good money at her job; what she didn't have was time to spend selling used clothes. So as soon as she had another armful of gorgeous little girl clothes that her daughter didn't fit in anymore, she trotted them down the street to the grateful neighbor with two tiny girls.

Meanwhile, sentimental me never gave my children's outgrown baby clothes to other moms. *All* of my children's clothes represented happy days and wonderful memories. Years later, when I was going through literally hundreds of outgrown sleepers, shirts, pants, dresses and coats that had been worn by my large family over the years, I realized how silly it had been to keep so many outgrown clothes in storage when they could have been used by other children all that time.

Clean-Sweepers Hate Clutter Just Like We Do

Yes, some clean-sweepers, like my mother and Kevin, seem pretty heartless. But most clean-sweepers understand that clutter piles up slowly and stealthily while we're busy with other things. They don't want a cluttered home, so they put up a front-line defense against clutter by moving things along just as soon as they're not useful anymore.

I imagine they occasionally regret getting rid of something too quickly. But their desire to keep a lid on the clutter must override their regret. That doesn't happen with those of us who tend to see value in too many things, but our willingness to keep everything certainly leaves us wallowing in stuff, and we don't like that, either.

That's why we need to take a page out of the clean-sweeper's book, and judge our possessions by whether they're still useful to us. If not, let's do something to keep the memories they represent, like taking a photo of them, and then move them on so someone else can get some use out of them. The lesson we sentimental types can learn from the clean-sweepers is that it's a lot easier to be generous to others if we don't hang on for dear life to everything we own, but instead let go of much of it so that others may benefit.

———◈———

Chapter 2 in a Nutshell

Clean-sweepers may not be sentimental, but they hate clutter like we do, and some of them can teach us a thing or two about helping others.

Chapter 3

Three Rules for Decluttering Success (for Sentimental People Only)

I imagine most clean-sweepers don't understand why there are books about decluttering. As far as they're concerned, what could be simpler than throwing away what you don't need? Or giving the good stuff to others and throwing out the rest?

That works for clean-sweepers. But for those of us who tend to be emotionally attached to our belongings, decluttering is a delicate process that often feels overwhelming and even frightening. At the very least, it looks like a process that requires more decision-making than we think we can handle.

But that doesn't mean it's impossible. You just need to know the three rules that must be followed during the decluttering process if you want your efforts to be a success. As long as those three rules are in force, you'll be well on your way to having a uncluttered home without a lot of regret over what you gave up to get it.

Rule 1: It Has to Go to a Good Home

We sentimental types have an easier time giving up things if we know they're going somewhere important, or to people who will really appreciate them. Just throwing everything in a dumpster, or putting it all out in boxes at the curb with "FREE" signs attached, is not going to work for items that we care about and have made a hard decision to give up.

We value all of our belongings; that's why we've kept them as long as we have. They've held our memories for many years. So we're not going to just throw away items that we consider to be valuable. They must go to good homes.

Even items that don't intrinsically trigger memories, but represent our hard work (or the hard work of a loved one) must be sent somewhere meaningful. If the item is an expensive one, just giving it away for a few dollars at a garage sale doesn't feel right. In that case, it's better to take the time to find a good market for the item or donate it where its value will be appreciated (see Anita's story later on in this book.)

For some of us, donating to thrift stores that help people with low incomes just by their existence makes us feel good. But for others, the Goodwill drive-up is not the best destination for our cherished belongings, and that's OK. It just means we'll have to work a little harder to find the right places to send those items.

Rule 2: The Memory Must Be Preserved

The main reason we sentimental types keep so many things is the memories they represent; we're afraid if we give up the items, we'll lose the memories.

While it's true that seeing saved items triggers memories, there are ways to look at those items without keeping them, so that they can trigger memories without taking up space and making you feel overburdened with stuff.

That's why it's so important to take photos of anything you're emotionally attached to before you let it go. You may never even look at the photos again, but you'll know you can if you want to. That knowledge takes away the anxiety of thinking that you'll never see those memory-laden items again. It's freeing to realize that you could lose your sentimental items in a fire or flood, but if you have digital photos of them, you can keep them forever.

As you go through your belongings, you may find items that once meant a lot to you but no longer do. Perhaps they represent an activity you were into, like rollerblading, or creating paintings, that you don't feel like doing again. Go ahead and take a photo of your old rollerblades or your best paintings anyways. Consider those photos examples of your personal history. After all, digital photos don't take up space, but years from now, you may get a kick out of seeing those reminders of who you once were.

If there are items that you think you really will want to look at all the time, keep their photos in a digital picture frame, or even create a collage wall out of them. Sites like **collagewall.com** make this especially easy.

Rule 3: It May Take Time

The usual goal of decluttering is to go through your entire house, get rid of every single unnecessary item, and end up with a clean, uncluttered home.

But this may not be possible for the sentimental person. It may take several rounds of decluttering over a period of time, maybe months, maybe years, before you can reach the point of living in a truly uncluttered home.

That's because the more sentimental you are, the more exhausting the decisions are, and you can only handle so many decisions before you burn out.

But it can be done. You may not be able to get rid of most of your excess possessions in the first go-round, but if you come back after a while, you'll probably find that you can get rid of more, because some of the items you kept no longer seem so necessary.

This is particularly true when it comes to the personal items of someone you've loved and lost to death. It takes time to grieve, and everyone grieves differently. Some people don't want any physical reminders of their loved one left around because seeing them is too painful. Others can't give up a single thing their loved one owned, not even a pair of socks. There is no right and wrong about this, but time resolves many of these issues.

So be patient with yourself as you go through this process. For the sentimental, decluttering is more likely to be a journey than a one-time event.

———✦———

Chapter 3 in a Nutshell

Sentimental people can achieve uncluttered homes, but only if they follow certain decluttering rules.

Chapter 4

Decluttering Your Home

Even though the process of decluttering your home is quite simple and basic, it's much more complicated for those of us who are sentimental, because unlike clean-sweepers, we keep tripping over our emotions.

It helps to stay focused on our mission, which is to reduce the number of belongings we keep in our homes. But when emotion takes over, it's easy to lose sight of this. Sometimes we focus on the wrong thing, as Krissy did when she drove home with a truckload of sentimental items and family heirlooms after her mother moved into a nursing home. As she drove, she kept thinking, "Where am I going to put all of this?" when what she should have been thinking is, "Which items will I keep? Which items will I give to family members? Which items should I donate to charity or sell? Which items belong in the dumpster?" Such truly helpful thoughts would be more likely to help her reach her goal of an uncluttered home.

It's important to keep *your* goal of a clean, uncluttered home foremost in your mind while keeping emotional thoughts at bay, if at all possible. Try to set aside truly sentimental items (to be dealt with later) while weeding out those items that don't mean as much to you. That builds momentum.

Also, think of what would happen if you lost everything in a flood or fire; you wouldn't have this chance to choose the very best items before giving up the rest.

We'll get into more strategies for going through sentimental items later in this book. For now, let's consider the basics of decluttering.

First off, you'll need to assemble some supplies:

- Gather together large plastic bags for trash, old boxes or plastic storage bins you don't need anymore for larger items you'll donate, and paper or plastic grocery bags for smaller items and clothes that you'll donate. You can also use these to transport items you're giving to someone else.

- Designate a special bin just for paper that you'll go through later; this includes personal correspondence, magazines, mail, kids' artwork, owner's manuals, receipts, etc.

- Get a large permanent marker that you'll keep in a designated spot so that you can label boxes and bins as you fill them.

- If you'll be going through a dusty, musty basement or attic, find some work gloves and a damp cloth or two.

Next, create a pleasant working environment:

- Put on some music to keep up your spirits.

- Turn off the volume on your phone so your decluttering momentum isn't interrupted.

- Brew a pot of coffee or tea and keep a mug-full (or a cold drink) near your work area.

- Choose a few places that aren't in sight of your work area to put items you will decide to give up. Foyers, stairs, utility rooms and garages are good temporary parking spots for clutter that's on its way out. Items to be donated can also go straight into your car's trunk or hatch. Move things into these areas regularly so that you're not tripping over stuff as you work.

- Choose a flat space in each room where you can sort through items and organize them. If there isn't one, make one by bringing in a card table or other small folding table. This is where you'll dump out a drawer you need to go through, or arrange a collection of small items so that you can easily see and choose the best (and get rid of the rest).

Now it's time to decide which decluttering method you will use. There are two primary methods for decluttering your home. Each has its pluses and minuses.

Method One: One Room at a Time

With this method, you work on one room at a time. You make decisions about what to give up and what to keep, one item at a time, and then you pitch the garbage and take the items you're giving up out of the room to a temporary parking spot, like the garage or the trunk of your car, until you can move them on. You then clean up and organize the room and its remaining contents. Some people go clockwise around the room; other people (like me) go back and forth between messy areas. It doesn't really matter as long as you get the room to being the best it can be, clutter-wise.

The good part of this method is that seeing the room in all its clean and spacious glory will be so inspiring that you'll be motivated to keep going on the rest of the rooms in your home.

The risky part of this method is that you're not likely to take the items you're getting rid of to their destinations each time you finish decluttering a room. That would mean a lot of trips! So you'll probably let it accumulate in your garage or basement, where you can see it regularly and maybe start rethinking some of your decisions. That's no good! You need to move things on promptly.

If you don't usually change your mind once it's made up, this method may work for you. But if you're the type that might have second thoughts when you see your belongings in the garage waiting to be sent away, you might want to try the next decluttering method instead.

Method Two: The Big Purge

This method requires a big burst of energy and excitement. You pick a day to begin decluttering and then you take a bag designated as Trash and go around the house pitching anything that's broken, anything that's actually garbage, and anything that you don't think anyone would want.

You fill as many bags as you can, then take them all to the dump. The resulting feeling of relief, and the sight of less junk, will motivate you to keep going.

So then you take another bag marked Donate and go through the house finding everything that you don't need or want anymore that's too good to throw away. Fill as many bags as you can and take them directly to your local thrift store, Goodwill drive-up or Salvation Army drop-off box.

Now you're really starting to feel good! You've jettisoned a fair amount of stuff, and the house is looking less cluttered. That's the good part of this method.

The danger of this method is that you might be tempted to stop here, because the house looks a lot better as long as you don't think about all those boxes in the basement, clothes in the closet and toys in the attic that include items you know you're personally attached to.

How to Choose?

Be honest with yourself. Which method sounds better to you, and more doable? That's the one to try first. But whichever method you choose, make a commitment to yourself to stick with the process until you've gone through your sentimental belongings, not just the items that are easy to donate or pitch.

Also, part of the process of decluttering is understanding that things will look worse before they get better. Sometimes you have to lay things out to see what you have, and that looks messy. You may have to stack or pile things on beds, table tops or even stair steps (an integral part of my basement decluttering efforts when we had our huge house years ago), and that looks even worse. Yes, it will look bad for a while, but it will get better. Just keep going and work through it. It will be worth it!

Are you wondering how you'll find time to declutter your home? Some people like the idea of dedicating five or ten minutes a day to decluttering, but that's never appealed to me, probably because I had so much stuff to go through. It does sound like a good plan for maintaining an uncluttered home, but if you've got a lot of belongings to go through, and some tough decisions to make, I think it's wise to set aside a day, a long weekend or even a week off to start work on this job. You need at least enough time to find and get rid of the easiest things to give up, go through the sentimental items and take as many as possible to the right destinations, and then put the house back together. The last thing you want is to run out of time when you have piles of stuff stacked all over the place.

What Worked for Me

In my case, we were under tight deadlines: to move out of a house, to get out of a storage unit, or to try and fit into a much smaller house. (As I said earlier, our decluttering process was spread out over our three moves in four years.) So it wasn't always possible to do things in an orderly fashion or work from room-to-room, and I was always under time pressure.

I found my decluttering rhythm by setting aside the items I was sentimental about as I found them, wherever I was working. That way I could keep going through the rest of our considerable amount of possessions without being overwhelmed by those tough decisions about sentimental items.

Once I had gone through the rest of the mess, having dispatched it all to one of three places (the next house, Goodwill or the dump), I was buoyed by the visual evidence of my success, especially seeing the nice, open empty spaces that resulted from my hard work. That gave me confidence to then tackle the sentimental items that required me to make some difficult decisions.

Do You Want Help?

Some people hate to declutter alone, and others prefer to do it alone. So having one or more helpers is a personal decision. Which do you prefer? Do you believe many hands make light work, or would you rather be the sole decision maker? It's up to you.

In my case, my husband was there to help me make the hard decisions. He had a vested interest, of course, because it was his back-breaking job to move boxes in and out of our various homes and storage units until we finally settled down in the little house we live in today. So he was definitely biased in favor of "Get rid of it!" when it came to most things. While he can be sentimental about some of his own things, like most men he saw no point in keeping every little thing from when our children were young, so he was instrumental in helping me keep only one small box of items for each child. Since the bulk of our clutter was kid-related, my husband's input was not only helpful, but necessary.

My younger children, who were teens at the time, did help by going through their own belongings and determining what to keep and what to give up. (I occasionally intervened.) They also moved boxes from one spot to another as needed and loaded our van with items to be donated to Goodwill. However, they were not involved in decision-making regarding household items. As for items belonging to my older children, who had already left home, we boxed those things up and gave them to our older kids when we saw them. What they chose to do with them was their problem, not ours. (I confess that I did keep a small box of my eldest son's baby items because I feared he would just pitch them all; I still have that box.)

Years ago, back when all of our kids were still living at home, and I had small decluttering sessions (which was all I had time for), I didn't want them anywhere near me because they always wanted to keep everything. So I paid the older ones to watch the little ones while I went through the basement and got rid of things. When I went through their bedrooms, where most of their favorite toys and other belongings were kept, I worked with them, not behind their backs. But those decluttering sessions were often contentious, and I'd come out of them exhausted after hours of negotiating which action figures could be given up, and which games were no longer being played with. And I always kept those toys, books and other items that I thought were too good to give up, or to which I was emotionally attached because they belonged to my children, even though *they* were willing to give them up. That's how we ended up with so much stuff when we were finally forced to declutter, years later.

If you tend to be emotionally attached to almost everything, you'll probably benefit from some help from your spouse or a friend (or two). But if you have many intensely personal items, including items that belong to a loved one who died, you may prefer to work alone. Ultimately, your personality along with the nature of your sentimental clutter will hold the key to whether you can or should do this by yourself, or not.

Choose Destinations Carefully and Quickly Dispatch Everything

During the decluttering process, once you've decided where your belongings should go, take them there as soon as you can. There are four reasons for this.

First of all, the sooner you move things along, the sooner you can enjoy an uncluttered home.

Second, if you leave boxes of outgoing items sitting around, even in your car, you'll be tempted to go through them again and keep one (or more) things after all, thus undoing all your hard work and good intentions.

Third, the sooner you give up those things, the sooner you'll forget about them. I'm not kidding! You may think you'll remember everything you gave up, but before long, you won't remember most of it.

Fourth, it's like ripping off a bandage. If you go slowly, you'll feel pain every step of the way. Do it fast and get it over with!

(That fourth step is the goal, of course, but the reality is that you may need more time to go through your most precious things. Fortunately, we change over time, and down the road it will become easier to let go of certain things than it may be right now.)

Keep in mind that trying to decide where to send things can slow you down and wreck your momentum. So before you get started on this process, think about where you would prefer to donate items. Are you content with the convenience of the Goodwill drive-up or the red Salvation Army drop-off box? Or would you rather donate to the local hospice thrift store, next week's animal shelter tag sale, or some other place that has more meaning to you? If you know where the excess is going ahead of time, you can just hop in the car and promptly get rid of the items you've culled out.

When You Get Bogged Down

When you get bogged down, and you probably will, try some of the following strategies:

- Take a break and leave the area where you're working; get a drink and a snack, and rest for a little while.

- Visualize what each area will look like without all the clutter: picture your big, roomy-once-again closet with shelves that have things sitting on them, not stacked up to the next shelf. Imagine your room with enough extra space that you can rearrange the furniture without having to move all sorts of stuff first. Perhaps you'll paint one wall or more to add some pizazz to the room, just because you can, now that you've gotten rid of so much clutter.

- If you're stumped when a room still looks cluttered after you've gone through it, think about your purpose for that room and determine which items don't contribute to that purpose. This may lead to the realization that certain items you kept don't really fit in with your decor, and that the room looks better without them. If you're emotionally attached to these items, take them out of the room and put them in the garage (or whichever area you're putting things until you can take them out of the house). Work somewhere else and then come back to those items later and consider how old they look and how they used to fit in with your old decorating taste, but not your current style. This may make it easier to let them go.

• Reconsider your decision about having help with the decluttering process. Is it possible that your helper is actually making things worse by questioning your decisions when you choose to get rid of something? On the other hand, if you chose to do this alone, is it possible that you need a friend to keep encouraging you as you work your way through this tough job? Adding or subtracting a helper may be just what you need to keep going until the job is done.

• Look at the time. Have you been working for hours? Maybe it's time to stop decluttering for the day. Take out the trash, move items you're donating or giving to friends and relatives to your garage or other temporary spot, and clean up the area where you've been working. Try to shut down operations before you're completely exhausted; that will help you stay motivated for your next decluttering session.

The Four Steps of Decluttering

Whether you decide to go through your home room by room or in one big purge, you'll need a system to categorize everything. Using trash bags marked Keep, Donate, Pitch and Sell is one way to do it. Putting those same labels on boxes will work, as will making a Keep pile, a Donate pile, etc. and then putting them in bags or boxes later on. How you do this doesn't matter that much; what's important is that you get the job done, so sort in whatever way seems best to you.

Sometimes, the room you're decluttering makes the decluttering technique obvious. If you're decluttering a bedroom, use the bed: put the keepers up by the pillows, the items to be donated at the foot of the bed, and the trash in a bag or box on the floor. If it's *your* bedroom, there's an added incentive in that you won't be able to go to sleep until the job is done and the bed is cleared.

If you're decluttering the basement, a table and/or the stairs can help you organize items as you go through them. If you have a lot of items, you may need to make a clearing in the room and put piles or bags there.

Please note: It's very important to remember that *the area you're working in will look a lot worse before it gets better*. Sorting looks messy; it can't be helped. So try not to let the sorting mess discourage you. Whenever you get to the point where you're starting to feel overwhelmed, move things you're not keeping out of the house. Pitch the trash and put the items to be donated in a temporary parking spot outside the house. This will really help you both mentally and in terms of having room to work.

Whether you've chosen to work on one room at a time, or you're doing one big purge, you're going to make a decision about everything in your path. Some things will go in the trash, some will be donated, some may be sold, and the rest will be kept for the time being. But you'll be going through those Keep piles again, later on. So let's get started!

Step 1: Pitch

Once you make the decision to declutter, the first step is the easiest: find and pitch the garbage.

So, what's garbage? It's:

- Newspapers, magazines and catalogs you meant to read but never did (recycle)

- Collections of margarine tubs, empty glass jars and lids (recycle)

- Old squashed-from-years-of-use scrub brushes, bath brushes and loofas

- Ripped, stained or threadbare towels, linens and throw rugs

- Old plastic bags and paper sacks (check inside first)

- Clothes that are badly stained, stretched out, have holes in them that can't be repaired and haven't been worn in a year (check the pockets first)

- Clothes and bedding that are badly stained, mildewed or moth-eaten (check the clothes' pockets first)

- Old wallets, briefcases and backpacks that you'd be too embarrassed to donate (check thoroughly first)

- Old socks, beat-up shoes and boots

- Old cans of paint (if dried up; otherwise send to environmentally safe disposal)

- Old appliance boxes

- Old make-up, half-used-then-forgotten shampoo or body-wash bottles, old medicines

- Paper gift bags that look very used

- Broken toys that cannot be fixed

- Broken sporting goods items, like bald basketballs and cracked baseball bats

- Broken furniture or décor items that can't be fixed

OK, so that wasn't too hard, right? Taking out the trash will help motivate you to keep going, because it feels so good to get useless things out of your way. But as the old song goes, we've only just begun.

Step 2: Donate

Items that go in the Donate box include things that aren't garbage but that you aren't attached to; they still have life left in them. Some people pitch such things, but most people don't want to throw perfectly usable items into landfills, so they donate them to a thrift store or good cause instead.

In this book, the Donate category also includes items that you're attached to but that you know you should move along so someone else can enjoy them. Remember, we sentimental types have an easier time giving up things if we know they're going somewhere meaningful. So if you have a pet cause, such as cancer research or animal rights, you can donate items to their rummage sales so that some or all of the proceeds go to help that cause. The list of good causes that sell donated items to raise funds includes:

- Animal Sanctuaries

- Cancer Societies

- Children's Homes

- Children's Hospitals

- Churches

- Crisis Pregnancy Centers

- Disabled Veterans' Centers

- Hospices

- Hospitals

- Humane Societies

- Parochial/Private Schools

- Senior Centers

- Women's Shelters

Thanks to the Internet, it's much easier than it used to be to find a great place for your donations:

- Put the name of your town and your favorite cause plus the phrase "thrift stores" or "rummage sales" into a search engine to get local results.

- Access a list of local thrift stores to see if any support one of your favorite causes by filling out the form at **thethriftshopper.com**

- Read this excellent article that explains how to find a true charity thrift store instead of a for-profit thrift store using a charity's name:

www.vcreporter.com/2010/02/the-truth-behind-thrift-stores-and-their-charities/

You can also donate specific items to charities where they will be used. For instance:

- Men's clothes can go to homeless shelters, Working Wardrobes, etc.

- Women's clothes can go to homeless shelters, battered women's shelters, Dress for Success, etc.

- Baby and children's toys and clothes are often needed at homeless shelters, daycare centers, crisis pregnancy centers, and foster care agencies.

- Household items like furniture and kitchenware can be used by group homes for people with special needs.

- Kitchen items are often needed by soup kitchens.

One benefit to donating is that it's environmentally responsible to reuse items instead of throwing them in landfills. But for the sentimental, knowing that beloved items are now helping others actually makes it easier to let go of them. For example, after Andy donated a large group of his possessions (including several items that were really hard for him to give up) to a fundraiser for a local rescue shelter, he said he felt so good about helping those animals that he just couldn't regret what he gave away.

If your items have historical value, but you have no one to give them to, consider donating them to a historical society or museum.

Note: If you want the tax deductions of whatever you donate, you'll have to keep track of everything, learn what it's all worth, and document it all. This prolongs the entire decluttering process; only you can decide if it's worth it to you.

Give Where It's Needed and Appreciated

While most thrift stores and some charities take almost anything, there may be better places for certain items to go. For example, if you've thought about giving items you inherited to someone in your family who would really appreciate them, why not do so now? Many young people don't really value heirlooms and other valuable items from the past, but some do.

That said, don't give anything to family or friends unless you know they really need or want it. You don't want to overwhelm them with your clutter. When in doubt, just ask them if they want the item. Text or email them a photo, too.

Often, the nature of an item will clue you in to someone in your family who could use it. Perhaps your late dad's trumpet, which has been sitting in your attic because you can't play it, would be appreciated by your young nephew, who recently began taking trumpet lessons. Or have you considered sharing those sundresses you wore in the 1970s (and would look silly in now) with your teenage neighbors? (Flower-child clothes are very hip again.)

If you're giving up something of value that you'd rather not just drop off at a donation center like Goodwill or Salvation Army, you can always group-text a photo of it to friends and family asking who wants it and specifying that the first one to pick it up gets it. That will keep the clutter moving out of your house and will make your job easier.

It also benefits you because directly helping a relative, friend or acquaintance by giving them something they want or need makes it much easier to let go of items you've treasured. And once those donated items are out of the house, you'll really start to see the difference in your home. Keep going!

Step 3: Sell

There may be many perfectly good things in your house that you no longer need or want, and that are worth enough money that you would like to try to sell. For instance, you may decide you're no longer attached to the 27 Waterford crystal goblets you got for your first wedding, the cigarette lighter collection your dad left you, and your autographed photo of a very young Mariah Carey. You can make some nice money selling sentimental items that other people collect, but it'll take time to do the research, learn the ropes, and pack and ship your items.

Try putting ads in the local newspaper or shopper, Blujay (**blujay.com**), craigslist (**craigslist.org**), eBay (**eBay.com**), or local Facebook community for-sale pages (**Facebook.com**). If you have a lot of items to sell, consider that Blujay lets you have an online shop for free, and then you can post your shop link to craigslist and Facebook. That way more people will see all the items you have for sale as well as those you specifically posted.

For large items like furniture, try putting them in your front yard with big signs showing the price. It can take time to sell things, but the cash you get for them will hopefully make it worth your time.

If you find a lot of items you no longer want that could be used to raise some cash, you can always have a garage or yard sale. Personally, I like going to garage sales, but having had several of my own over the years, I'd rather have a root canal than host one more garage sale. It's an awful lot of work. But maybe you're up for it. If so, I hope you make a nice chunk of change! (Be sure to advertise your sale on

Bookoo (**bookoo.com**) and craigslist, mentioning specific items you have for sale that someone might find during a search of those sites; they'll serve as keywords.)

Garage sales are great for moving along items you don't need or care about anymore, but I really, really don't recommend that you sell your truly sentimental items in a garage sale. For one thing, it's way too easy to reconsider your decision to part with things when you see them again in order to set up a sale.

It's also very painful to see your precious things being pawed through by strangers; having someone low-ball you on something you loved is like pouring salt in the wound. Years ago, I had a garage sale to sell off my children's baby clothes and toys after my doctor told me it would be risky for me to get pregnant again (I later switched doctors and had more kids, but that's another story). I vividly recall a woman who persistently negotiated me down to five cents each for the like-new undershirts that my newborn babies only wore for a short time. It wasn't the money that kept me going back and forth with her; it was the fact that I was still emotionally attached to those little white snap-front shirts. Do you really want to argue with someone over how much your beloved M.C. Hammer "Hammerman" lunchbox (the one you took to school all through fifth grade) is worth?

Finally, having things left over after a garage sale, precious things that were rejected by strangers all day, doesn't feel very good either. So my recommendation is to sell only items you no longer need or want at a garage sale.

(Many people don't like the idea of selling their sentimental items, so if you have no *unwanted* items worth cash, just skip this step altogether.)

Step 4: Keep

Now that you've reduced some clutter and are buoyed by how good it feels to get rid of extra stuff, you're ready to tackle the things you've chosen to keep.

Before we get started, let's get one thing clear: when you were going through your home, I assume you didn't put *everything* you wanted to keep in the Keep pile. For instance, your televisions most likely stayed put, and you probably didn't take every picture off the walls to put in the Keep piles. And that's fine because I'm not asking you to choose between your forks and your spoons; I'm assuming that you'll keep every item that you still like and actually use for daily living.

From here on out, when I refer to your Keep pile, I'm referring to the items you decided to keep that you don't see or use regularly: things you've collected, things that were in drawers or closets or boxes, things that overflowed your shelves and other display areas, and things you've kept out of sight.

These are the items that were left after you pitched the junk and donated or sold the usable stuff, yet they are not the items you use on a daily basis. They are *everything else you kept.*

Consider this the danger phase of decluttering for sentimental types. We don't have much problem giving up garbage, and since we see value in unwanted-but-unbroken things, we can usually find items to donate in general terms or give to specific people who might need or want them.

But the Keep boxes, piles or bags represent our step into deep waters, because until now we've always found far, far too many things to keep. That's how we ended up in a cluttered house. We struggle with giving up these items, usually because we're sentimental about them in one way or another. So this is where the going gets tough.

For that reason alone, Step 4 gets its own chapter. But before we get there, I want to ask you a question. Have you ever been to an estate auction?

At an estate auction, someone's belongings collected over a lifetime are hauled out of their home and spread out on tables that can cover the entire yard. These are all things that someone felt were very valuable, or had great sentimental meaning to them, or were too special for everyday use, so they sat in a box somewhere in that home for years, even decades.

When the auction begins, the auctioneer will go from table to table, auctioning off each item. Some items will be sold individually, while others will be sold in a group. Items that don't sell will be tossed in a box with others that didn't sell and will finally go for a few bucks for the whole box. Time is of the essence because there are so many tables full of stuff waiting to be sold off, so the auctioneer will charge steadily from table to table, letting things go for next to nothing at times just to get them off the tables.

Going to an estate auction can be a real wake-up call regarding how valuable a person's belongings actually are. So when you keep something packed away because it's special, and too good to use because it might break or fade, *you may be preserving it so that it can someday be sold to a stranger for a few dollars, if that.* Precious items you plan on passing down to your heirs may end up in the trash someday, if your heirs don't value them like you did (which is entirely possible).

When you put away items for "someday," or to keep them safe for your heirs, you cheat yourself and others out of the opportunity to use and appreciate those items right now. So when you go through your Keep piles, try hard to be practical instead of defaulting to your sentimental nature.

———⊰⊙⊱———

Chapter 4 in a Nutshell

The four-step decluttering process is pretty straightforward, but that fourth step is a doozy for sentimental people.

Chapter 5

Going Through Your Keep Piles

Keeping things was fine during the first go-round of decluttering, but anything you felt conflicted about or wanted to hang onto even though you didn't need it probably ended up in the Keep pile. So you most likely kept far more items than you have room for.

There's nothing wrong with keeping a few sentimental items. The problem is that some of us are *so* sentimental that almost anything can be a sentimental item to us. So we aren't selective when it comes to sentimental items: we keep them all! Then we become overwhelmed by the clutter that results.

This is probably a familiar pattern, but it's time to break that habit. You can't keep all of those items that survived the first round of decluttering, but you don't have to get rid of them all, either.

(Some decluttering advocates make you feel as though you must get rid of every extra possession that doesn't serve a daily purpose in order to have a truly decluttered home. That's nonsense!)

Instead of planning to get rid of *everything*, which strikes fear in the hearts of us sentimental types, you can group your sentimental items and then prioritize them. Reducing your possessions while keeping the items that are most precious to you is a matter of choosing your favorites in each category of sentimental items and giving up the rest. (Remember, by taking digital photos of every sentimental item you give up, you won't feel like those memories are lost forever.) This is what you'll be doing with all of your sentimental items.

Then, instead of packing away the items you decide to keep, you'll use or display most of them. One of the gifts we sentimental types have is the ability to find items that warm our hearts while personalizing our homes. The problem arises when we find and keep far too many of those items. By keeping and displaying only your most beloved belongings, you can make your home special without making it cluttered.

So, instead of just going through your sentimental items one by one, this time around you're going to group them into categories and then rank the items in each category. Categories include:

- Books
- Babies' and kids' clothes, toys, artwork and schoolwork
- Heirlooms, inherited belongings, and possessions of late loved ones
- Gifts and other expensive items

- Collections
- Items that represent a lost dream
- Memories and mementos from our youth
- Clothes, accessories and footwear
- Video games
- Craft supplies
- Movies
- School books and papers (includes college)

The first seven categories on the list are common enough and complex enough that I call them the Sentimental Seven, and we'll go into them in more detail later in this book. But these categories (and however many more you might come up with) all lend themselves to prioritizing, which is exactly what we're going to do.

From here on out, the process of decluttering involves picking a category, finding everything you've kept that falls into that category, and looking at the entire group with an eye to ranking its items from your most favorite to your least favorite.

This may require laying out all the items in a category on tables so you can see them all at once, or doing the job in a specific space (like decluttering your sewing supplies and fabric in your sewing room). Whatever it takes, commit to reducing one category at a time; try not to start a new category until you've finished with the previous one.

Two Parameters That Will Help You Prioritize Your Belongings

The 19th century British artist and writer William Morris once said:

> "Have nothing in your house that you do not know to be useful, or believe to be beautiful."

This quote offers two basic parameters for decluttering. The first one, being useful, is objective and therefore easier to implement. Either something is useful or it's not. If it's broken and not repairable, it's not useful. If it's in fine shape but you don't need it, it's not useful to you. Whether or not something is useful is pretty clear-cut.

It's that second parameter that's a little trickier, because it's subjective; after all, beauty is in the eye of the beholder. That explains why, when your husband refers to your much-loved Beanie Baby collection as ratty, you feel shocked and angry. When you look at those colorful beanbag creatures, you recall being the young girl who collected them, and you remember how much you loved them, the excitement every time you got a new one, the thrill to be the first kid at school to have one....you don't really notice that they look as though they've had a lot of handling, er, loving, because you're looking at them through eyes of love.

Since we sentimental people see beauty in everything we love, that second parameter is one that's easily manipulated.

Nevertheless, when you're trying to choose amongst your belongings, trying to decide on what to keep and what to pass along, keep that quote in mind, but add two words:

> "Have nothing in your house that you do not know to be useful, or believe to be **the most** beautiful."

This is where prioritizing comes in. Which of your belongings give you *the most* pleasure whenever you see them? Which are your very most precious keepsakes, the ones you would regret losing *the most* if your house or storage unit burned down, the ones that you can't imagine letting go of? All of your things are beautiful to you; that's why you've kept them thus far, maybe even moved them from apartment to apartment or from house to house. But be honest with yourself: there's a core group of items that are *the most* precious, *the most* beautiful, and *the most* important to you. Those are the items you will find and keep.

Implicit in Morris' statement is the idea that you'll put your beautiful items where you can see them. After all, what good is beauty if you can't see it and appreciate it? That's why the most beautiful items you own, the ones that mean the most to you, the ones you will decide (after prioritizing) to keep, should remain visible to you in some form from now on.

So as you proceed with the decluttering process, setting aside your "most beautiful" things and preparing to let go of the rest, don't just pack those most beautiful things back up in boxes and hide them again. Put your most beautiful items where you can see them and enjoy them.

If you'd rather store them away again and rarely look at them, maybe they aren't really your "most beautiful" things after all. In that case, why let them take up precious space? It will be easier to look at a photo of them than to go into the attic or basement, move all the boxes around as you dig through them trying to find the right item, and then put it all back together when you're through. You know you're not going to do that, right? So why even have all this stuff? Again, keep only that which is "most beautiful," and put it where you can see it and enjoy it every day. Take photos of almost-as-beautiful items so you can see them when you want to, and then let the items go. If you do this, your house will be made beautiful by your most beautiful items, yet it will also be uncluttered because you let go of all but *the most* beautiful.

Be aware that second thoughts are all part of the prioritizing process. An item that you believe is very important to you but that you're willing to relegate to a box in the back of the crawlspace probably doesn't rank as highly as you think. On the other hand, an item that you decide to let go of with *deep* regret should probably be moved up higher in the rankings instead of moving it along.

One way to clarify your thoughts is to consider what you would do if your place caught fire. What would you save? Of course, you wouldn't be able to save much, if anything. What would you replace? What would you even remember? Many of these sentimental items are things you haven't even thought about in ages because they've been packed away. You've lived without seeing them daily until now; don't you think you'd survive without them in the future if they were lost in a fire? That's why you can cut loose anything now that you couldn't replace after a fire.

Choosing Your Most Beautiful Things

If you were looking at a packed football stadium full of people, it would be very hard to pick your spouse or your child out of the crowd. But if you were at a family gathering of a dozen people, you'd spot them very quickly.

The same principle holds true for your most special treasures, the belongings that you don't ever want to give up. If they're part of your houseful of packed-away possessions, buried deep inside one of many, many boxes in your attic, basement, or crawlspace, it will take quite an effort to see them (that goes double if they're in a storage unit). Even if they're part of a large collection that you've displayed, like your favorite childhood baseball or Pokemon card that's one of 200+ cards in framed groups covering the long wall of your family room, they're not very noticeable individually.

If you want to be able to truly enjoy your *most* treasured and important possessions, you must 1) put them out where you can see them, and 2) not surround them with a host of like items. To live an uncluttered life with your most treasured possessions, you must keep far fewer of them. Make the effort to choose only the very best and most special of your belongings, let go of the rest, and then display the chosen few where you can always see and enjoy them. The beloved items you keep will have more room to shine if there's no clutter around them.

Choosing the best of the bunch means making choices, which can be quite painful (especially once you've gotten rid of the easiest things to give up and are left to choose among the most beloved). But the more you keep, the less you'll be able to appreciate what you actually kept. And by keeping only the very best and then putting them where you can see them (or regularly use them), you honor them far more than you did by burying them in boxes in your attic or basement where you never saw them.

How Many Items Should You Keep?

After you group your belongings into categories (ex. books from college, your late mom's belongings), go through one group at a time, arranging items in order of their importance to you. Decide how many items you will keep from each group, and *allow yourself more items from the more important groups*. For example, you might choose to keep only three books from college, but 10 of your late mom's belongings.

Reserve the top three or ten or however many items from each group and take the rest out of the house to your garage or car. Go back in the house and look at what's left; do you have room to put these items where you can see and enjoy them? If not, remove the least important from each group. Keep going until you're left with only your very most important items.

The number of items you keep depends not only on how much space you have, but also on how large the items are. For instance, I kept about 24 pairs of earrings and gave up several dozen that I hadn't worn in years. I also kept dozens of books, enough to fill three bookcases. But I gave away or donated several hundred books. In fact, while we kept six bookcases (we also store DVDs on them), we gave away or sold several more, because once we gave up a lot of books, we didn't need so many bookcases.

Three bookcases take up a lot more space than even 100 pairs of earrings, so clearly your choice of how many of a given item to keep depends on its physical size. It also depends on whether you still really need or want any of them. If I had let the piercings in my ears close up, I could have given up *all* of my earrings. If you were once a tole painter but lost interest in it, there would be no need to keep even just your favorite paintbrushes. So get rid of an entire category or group if it no longer interests you and if, deep down, you know you aren't going to use it again. ("I might use it again someday" is a handy excuse for keeping something instead of dealing with it, so be honest with yourself.)

You can always *use a specific storage space to help you limit how much you keep.* For instance, you could put your most treasured items in a decorative box or in an antique suitcase. Keep only what will fit inside while allowing you to close the box or suitcase.

To make things really simple, *keep only the best three items in each group*: the best three hats, the best three necklaces, the best three knick-knacks. In some groups, you may not even have three items left. Great! That means fewer decisions to make.

Again, you don't need to keep a lot of any one group. Just a few items can trigger happy memories, but too many items become a burden.

Where Will You Keep Your Most Beautiful Items?

Remember the Morris quote: useful and beautiful. You must be able to see something to appreciate its beauty, so where will you keep your best belongings instead of storing them away in boxes?

Think about where you'll display the items in each category while you're prioritizing them. Suppose you want to keep six of your favorite painstakingly-assembled-by-your-little-fingers model cars from childhood: where will you put them? Perhaps you decide to arrange them on top of a bookcase or on a shelf, but there's only room for five cars. You know what to do: give up your least favorite of the six.

Large collections may require a chosen destination *before* you decide how many to keep. For example, I had dozens of cookbooks before I moved to my current (small) home, but I only kept seven favorites because that's all that would fit on the half-a-shelf I had available in the kitchen.

Don't keep any collections unless you have a definite destination for them. The exception to the rule? In the case of small, very precious keepsakes that don't lend themselves to display, put them in a decorative box that you can easily access whenever you get the urge to go through them; perhaps the box can go in a dresser drawer, or in your closet. But the rest of your most beautiful items need specific destinations where they'll be on display, or out they go.

How to Sort and Set Priorities While Decluttering

When you put a limit on yourself of how many items you can keep, you force yourself to set priorities. This will help you admit that you don't need to keep nearly as many things as you have in the past. Deanna's situation illustrates this concept.

Deanna has always worked in corporate offices. Back in the 1980s, that meant she wore suits and dresses, most of them with big shoulder pads. During the 1990s, when dress slacks became more fashionable in offices than dresses, Deanna cultivated a lovely designer wardrobe of slacks. After 2000, when business casual came into vogue, she added a wide array of tops, cotton sweaters and cropped pants to her wardrobe.

Deanna kept *all* of these clothes, reasoning that the classics are always in style. As a result, every closet in her house is full of her clothes. There's also a rack in the cedar closet she had built in her basement years ago that holds many beautiful wool suits, sweaters and long winter coats. Deanna's house literally holds several hundred pieces of clothing; that estimate doesn't even include her vast shoe and boot collection.

But Deanna has almost reached retirement age, and she dreams of moving to Arizona so she can play golf all year round. Having visited friends there many times, she's already picked out the town she wants to live in and can visualize the condo she hopes to buy, with a balcony overlooking the pool.

As her retirement date looms larger, her vast wardrobe begins weighing on her mind; one night she even dreams that she's climbing over a towering mountain of her clothes to get to Arizona. But every time she tries going through one of her closets, and she sees the high-quality fabrics, the tasteful styles, the attractive prints and colors...well, she becomes overwhelmed and goes off to do something easier.

If Deanna truly wants to downsize to an Arizona condo near the golf course, she'll have to declutter her entire house, paring her possessions down to what will fit in a condo. That means she'll have to categorize and prioritize her beloved wardrobe, because she certainly can't take it all, or even most of it, with her. How will she do this?

First off, she'll need to pull out anything that looks dated. Even though she made an effort to buy classics over the years instead of trendy items, the fact is that collars, lapels, sleeves and pant-leg widths and lengths vary over the years. Items that once looked classic to Deanna now look like the 20- or 30-year-old items they are, even though she kept them in beautiful shape. If there's a dated-looking item that she thinks she'll still wear, she can set it aside for later consideration.

Weeding out the dated items should bring down the wardrobe by one-third to one-half. That's progress! She should avoid thinking about the amount of money those clothes represent and instead focus on how much she enjoyed wearing them back in the day. They served her well when she needed them, but times change. Her current lifestyle certainly hasn't required a pink peplum suit with highly padded shoulders and a big white faux chrysanthemum sewn to the lapel, for example, and it won't be suitable for life on the golf course, either.

The next step is to weed out what doesn't fit. Deanna has managed to keep a fairly steady weight all these years, but unfortunately, one of the worst symptoms of aging is that the weight tends to move around over time. She no longer has the tiny waist she had in her 20s and 30s, and it's unlikely that she will ever have it again. Once she admits that to herself, it will be easier to give up most of her dress slacks, especially those that are older than her two adult sons. Some of her dresses and suits are too short and can also be removed. Other items just don't fit properly anymore, so they too fail to stay in the keep pile. (An exception to this rule is if there are any particularly lovely items made of good fabric in a classic color. Deanna can take those to a tailor or dressmaker to see if any can be let out or taken in after replacing the giant shoulder pads with more reasonably-sized ones. Old clothing is often better-made than what you can buy in stores today, and has enough fabric in the seam allowances to make tailoring easy. Only do this if the item still suits your current lifestyle.)

Finally, Deanna has to pull almost all of the winter clothes, including coats, heavy sweaters and silk-lined wool slacks. She certainly won't need them in Arizona.

So let's recap how to go through an enormous wardrobe of much-loved clothes:

- Get rid of anything that looks dated (be honest!) Only keep something if you're certain you'll wear it again.

- Get rid of anything that doesn't fit. Yes, you might lose weight. But when you lose weight, you'll probably buy new clothes to celebrate, right?

- Get rid of anything that no longer works for your lifestyle. If you've gone from stay-at-home mom to employed mom, get rid of the sweats and grungy, stained tops. If you gave up horseback riding, pass the jodhpurs along. If you're retiring to Arizona, ditch the full-length down jackets.

This should reduce the number of clothes down to a much more reasonable figure. In Deanna's case, she is left with only two closets' worth of clothes: certainly not enough to create a mountain blocking her way to Arizona, but still more clothes than she will need.

So Deanna is ready for step 4: prioritizing. She divides her clothes into piles of dresses and skirts, slacks, jeans and tops. Then she pulls her five favorites from each pile. She then determines which items go best with others, making any needed changes in her priorities as she goes along.

After doing this, she's left with a modest-sized wardrobe that consists of her very favorite clothes. She knows she'll need more warm-weather clothes, but that can be remedied once she moves to Arizona.

She keeps only two dated items that she truly loves. One is a wool fisherman's sweater she bought in Ireland while on vacation many years ago. The quality is top-notch and it's the warmest sweater she's ever owned. She figures that if she never wears it in Arizona, she'll have a pillow made out of it for her sofa.

The second item is a polka-dotted maternity dress she wore while pregnant with her sons. It's long past its sell-by date, but there are just too many good memories in that dress. She figures she'll hang it in the back of her closet and it will make her smile whenever she sees it.

In the end, Deanna ends up with one closet's worth of clothes and a lot of empty closets. What a relief! But there's just one problem; the beds in her boys' old room are stacked high with clothes she decided to give up. She knows she needs to move them on quickly before she's tempted to keep some of them after all.

A friend recommends a couple of upscale consignment stores where Deanna's excess clothes might be appreciated and sold for good money. Two carloads later, the extra clothes are gone. Each month, Deanna will receive a check in the mail for the items that sell. Anything that doesn't sell within six months will be donated to the local hospice's thrift shop.

At times, Deanna experiences an occasional twinge when she remembers all the nice clothes she gave up. But a walk past one of her empty closets eases the pain remarkably, and she has yet to have another "clothes mountain" dream.

Deanna's decluttering success came once she made the decision to sort through everything, using the steps of:

- Removing what's so out of date that you'll never wear it again,

- Removing what doesn't fit,

- Removing what's no longer appropriate for your lifestyle, and prioritizing what's left.

This is a cut-and-dried process for a pragmatic, unsentimental person. But for sentimental people like Deanna and you and me, it's a process that's full of nostalgia, so it's harder for us, and it takes longer. But having those steps is a big help.

More Strategies for Prioritizing Your Sentimental Items

Different collections of sentimental items may require different steps to prioritize them. You now know the steps to use when going through your personal wardrobe. Let's look at strategies for prioritizing groups of other much-loved items.

When looking at a group of sentimental items, consider first: **which items can be replaced in a way that takes up less space?**

- You can replace record albums and tapes with digital files.

- You can replace books with eBooks.

- You can scan artwork and turn it into digital files.

- You can convert home-recorded videotapes into DVDs or digital files.

- You can scan old photos and convert them into digital files.

You'll find more details on these specific items in the "Collections" section of Chapter 6. Thanks to technology, many of the things we've kept that take up space can be replaced and saved on our computers and other digital devices instead, saving us a lot of space in the process.

Another thing you can do when going through items you're emotionally attached to is to ask yourself **which items are in bad shape?** Perhaps you saved your favorite childhood sweater, but it looks like moths got to it here and there. Take a photo and then throw it away, because you can't give a moth-eaten sweater to any child, whether they're related to you or they get it via your anonymous donation.

Try to look at your belongings with the eyes of a stranger to determine which items are in bad shape. Anything full of holes or tears, anything that's going to pieces, anything that's missing integral parts that you can't replace...these are candidates for being thrown away. When you find an old board game that's missing half the pieces, pitch it. When you discover an old Barbie doll that's missing half her hair or one of her bendable legs, let her go. It's amazing how many of what we remember as treasured items are really junk because they're in tatters or faded, but we never realized it because we look at them through eyes of love. But when it's in such bad shape that you can't even donate it, you need to throw it out. Again, if you're worried about losing the memories, take photos first. It's better to have a lot of photos of sentimental items in bad shape in your camera or phone than a lot of actual sentimental items in bad shape in your house.

Finally, ask yourself: **what do I have that I don't use but still has useful life in it?** This includes furniture, appliances, clothing and shoes that are classic and in good shape. You may have already donated such items when you first began decluttering, but now we're talking about the things you set aside with your sentimental items. Admit it: you love them, you remember them, but you never use them.

In my case, this included my children's old high chair, the big and cumbersome red Little Tikes car my younger children loved, and board games the entire family played. These are just the things that I can still recall. I know that there were many other items I loved and had kept for many years that I finally gave up. I hope the fact that I can't remember most of them anymore comforts you: seriously, the more sentimental clutter you give up, the more you won't remember after a while.

Ultimately, you have to ask yourself why you keep things you don't use anymore when they could be used and enjoyed by someone else, particularly someone less fortunate. Donate them and let the knowledge that you helped someone ease your sadness at giving up things you used to love. (Charities like Dress for Success have clients who can't afford good clothes for their job searches; your beloved old dress clothes could really make the difference for someone.)

Asking yourself these questions will winnow out lesser items, leaving you with the cream of the crop.

Useful and Beautiful

Occasionally you'll find that some items you consider to be beautiful can also become useful to you, thus fulfilling both of William Morris' rules. That's how things worked out for Ed.

Ed will tell you he's not a sentimental guy: that as a police sergeant, he can't afford to be sentimental. But his wife Melissa will tell you that he's nuts. Her reason? His closet and drawers are overstuffed with shirts, but to Melissa's great frustration, he won't give up even one of them.

Since Ed wears a uniform at work, he really only needs a casual wardrobe for his off-hours, and a suit for those times when he has to make a court appearance. So what's filling up his closet, his side of the dresser, and some large plastic bags in the spare room? T-shirts, over 200 of them.

There are t-shirts from his favorite bands from back in the day, and t-shirts from concerts he attended. There are t-shirts from marathons he has run, and t-shirts from local charitable events he's attended as part of his job. There are even t-shirts from his high school years.

Melissa is sick of having the t-shirts stashed everywhere, considering he doesn't even wear them anymore. She offered to start making them disappear while he's at work, figuring he wouldn't remember them anyways, but he was appalled and told her in no uncertain terms that he was keeping them all.

Melissa was at her wits' end because she couldn't come up with a solution they could agree on. But Ed's brother Benny unwittingly helped her out when he stopped by one day to brag to Ed about his latest acquisition.

Holding out his phone to Ed, Benny said, "Hey bro, check out my bed!"

Ed looked at the photo and said, "Big deal."

"You don't like it?" Benny asked in a hurt tone.

"What *is* it?"

"It's a t-shirt quilt, you moron. All my favorite shirts from the good old days, keepin' me warm again."

Ed looked dubious, but his curiosity was clearly piqued.

"How'd you do it?"

"This chick who lives in my building makes these things and sells 'em. You give her all your shirts and a couple hundred bucks, she gives you a quilt. Come on, you gotta see it!"

So Ed hopped on the back of Benny's motorcycle and they roared off down the street.

An hour later, Ed was back home and busy pulling t-shirts out of his dresser drawers when Melissa found him. She could barely conceal her joy at seeing all those t-shirts being stuffed into trash bags.

"What's going on, Ed?"

"Benny has a bedspread made out of his old t-shirts and it's so cool. I talked to the girl who made it and she thinks she can make me two since I have so many shirts....she said if I bring 'em over right away she'll start working on 'em tomorrow!"

For once, Melissa was at a loss for words. Such mixed emotions! Joy at getting rid of all the t-shirts, and nausea at the thought of their bed covered with them forever. But for Ed, it was the perfect solution. Now Melissa could quit nagging him about the t-shirts, and he could have a nice, warm, soft cover made of all his memories. As soon as he'd seen and felt Benny's t-shirt quilt, he knew he had to have one of his own. And he was getting two!

The t-shirt quilt might not have been Melissa's ideal solution, but for Ed and indeed for most people, a t-shirt quilt is a way to keep their most precious memorable clothes in a form that they can see and use. This is a great solution for handling sentimental memories represented by physical items: re-purposing them into something new and useful that you will see regularly.

Here are some more examples of sentimental items that have been made useful *and* beautiful:

- Laurel's husband died after a long battle with leukemia, and she was left with a closet full of the plaid shirts he always wore. She decided to make seven quilts, one for each of their children, using those shirts. She worked through her grief as she sewed, and her children were thrilled with their quilts made of plaid rectangles that reminded them of their dad.

- Someone in our old neighborhood (a historic district) lined their large trees with borders made of Grandma's old china dinner plates.

- Anna's late mother-in-law always wore brightly colored polyester slacks. Not wanting to harm the environment by sending practically indestructible polyester items to a landfill, Anna cut the slacks into strips and made a lovely braided rug that reminds her and her family of Ma.

- Thomas' beloved late grandmother was known for her flamboyant personal style that included the wearing of many ornate and valuable rings. He inherited several of them and put them on display on his coffee table, after buying an old department-store hand display model at an antique shop and covering it with the rings. It makes quite a conversation piece when friends visit, and he is happily reminded of his grandmother whenever he looks at it.

Regarding that last example, people often inherit jewelry that they hate to give up but aren't going to wear. Remember that you can buy a shadow box, line it with fabric and display the best pieces of jewelry; buying a glass-topped table to display the jewelry safely is another option. The jewelry then becomes part of your decor.

In the case of larger items, like furniture, sometimes you can re-purpose a beloved item into something you need. For example, perhaps you don't need another bed in your house, but you love your dad's old headboard and bed frame and hate to give it up. You can turn it into a bench for your empty foyer, or a porch swing for your covered front porch; I've seen many examples of this on **Pinterest.com**. Maybe your great-aunt's ornate iron sewing machine base can be turned into a lovely end table or plant table. Think of what you need and how one of your sentimental items might actually serve that purpose. You'll get to keep something you love and save money in the process by not buying a new bench, swing, end table or plant table.

———⋙◉⋘———

Chapter 5 in a Nutshell

Distilling down your "Keep" piles is the key to conquering your sentimental clutter.

Chapter 6

The Sentimental Seven

We sentimental types have trouble giving up almost anything that has meaning to us. But there are seven categories of items that are particularly challenging for us to give up. They're also the most common groups of items that people tend to keep too much of in their homes. They are:

- Books
- Babies' and kids' clothes, toys, artwork and schoolwork
- Heirlooms, inherited belongings, and possessions of late loved ones
- Gifts and other expensive items
- Collections
- Items that represent a lost dream
- Mementos of our youth

Let's take a look at strategies for dealing with items in the each of the Sentimental Seven.

Books

For most people, books are like old friends. But for sentimental people, books remind us of who we used to be, how old we were when we discovered a certain book, the interests we had when we bought a certain book...in other words, books are intertwined with our lives. That's one reason why it's very hard to give them up, even if we don't feel like reading some of them anymore. In fact, the irony is that while we may have hundreds of books in our homes, we usually buy or borrow something new when we have an urge to read something.

It's hard to think of books as clutter, but they do take up lots of space and we tend to keep them long after we're done with them. So technically, too many books *is* clutter.

Of course, unlike old clothes, old decorative items, old kitchenware and the like, you can never throw out a book. If there isn't a law against it, there should be, because books are treasures. That said, they also weigh a lot, take up lots of room in packing boxes when you move, collect dust and become musty and even moldy if you store them in a basement or (horrors!) a storage unit that isn't climate controlled.

To complicate things further, when you're going through your books, trying to figure out which ones to let go of, it's very easy to get caught up in an old favorite. The next thing you know, you're several chapters in and still surrounded by piles of books you haven't sorted through yet.

No wonder the idea of finding books to give up creates great anxiety in sentimental people like us!

I think book collections (i.e. our personal libraries) are hugely sentimental because they reflect the varying interests we've had during our lives. In the case of fiction, we also tend to associate certain beloved stories with our past. For example, when I reread *Gone with the Wind*, I'm 13 all over again. That's how old I was when I discovered the tumultuous love story of Scarlett and Rhett, set during and after the Civil War. A good friend loaned me her copy of the book and we would talk about it at length. So my memories of her (she passed away many years ago) also come flooding back when I read *Gone with the Wind*. It's a huge book, well over 1,000 pages, so it takes up a fair amount of space. I recently got the eBook version of the novel, so I plan to take a photo of the copy I've owned for so many years before giving it up.

It's easy to say "Just buy the eBook" in order to save physical space while keeping a book in your virtual library. But what about those readers (and you know who you are) who write in books? The things you've written in them make them more personal, and even like diaries, in a way, if you expressed your thoughts or opinions on the margins of books that you found thought-provoking. You can see how that complicates the eBook argument.

Then there are the memories associated with how you got a book. Maybe it was given to you (and signed on the flyleaf) by a beloved family member or friend. Perhaps you had to buy it for a college class and ended up loving the class and the book. Or perhaps you were a young girl who owned a grand total of three Nancy Drew detective novels, given to you by a favorite aunt who had kept them from her childhood. And one day someone on the next block had a garage sale, and you happened to be riding past on your bike. You saw the box filled with hardcover books bound in the familiar blue-green fabric, with a sign that said $5, which was a fortune back when your allowance was 30 cents a week. You rode home as fast as you could, busted up your ceramic Uncle Sam bank and stuffed five wrinkly dollar bills in your pocket, then rushed back to the garage sale before someone else could buy your treasure. Then you walked your bike home as you lugged the box. Once home, you reverently lined up all two dozen of your "new" Nancy Drews in a row on your bed's headboard/bookshelf, and thought you would never again be quite as happy as you were at that moment.

Yes, that was me, and I took those Nancy Drew books with me into adulthood, into all our different homes, rejoiced when my daughters read them and loved them, and then brought them to this little house and kept them here, for a while (I'll elaborate on that shortly). But the reality is that we just can't keep everything we're sentimentally attached to, and that includes books.

But we can tackle this challenge in the same way as other forms of sentimental clutter, er, items. First off, we need to go through our personal library and Pitch, Donate, Sell and Keep.

Which books do you pitch? Any that are moldy, of course, and any that you've written personal thoughts in that you don't want to keep, but also don't want to share.

Otherwise, there are better places to send the books you don't want.

As you go through the books, start sorting them: those you want to keep, those you don't want but think you can sell for a few dollars (or more), and those that you can easily give up. This last category includes:

- duplicates

- books that no longer interest you or that you weren't interested in enough to finish

- books related to past hobbies or other activities you no longer pursue

- reference books and textbooks that are now outdated. (We can find so much current information on the Internet nowadays that many reference books quickly become outdated or unnecessary.)

This part is easy and keeps the momentum going. Get these books out of your way and out to the car or other place you're putting them until you can donate them. This will leave more space to go through the rest of the books.

Now it will get harder. You'll find books that you love, of course, but your love of books is how you got into this mess in the first place, so remind yourself that you can't keep all of the books, and then consider people you know who might enjoy them.

One way to minimize the pain of giving up treasured books that you don't have room for is to give them to friends to read. It's like loaning them a book except that you don't expect to get it back. Do you see any books that might be particularly appreciated by a friend or loved one? I'm not talking about weighing people down with books because you'll feel better giving them to a friend than dropping them off at the Salvation Army or your local Goodwill store. But if you used to do calligraphy, and you know someone who still does it and might like the books, why not offer them your calligraphy books? Or if you used to love a certain novel or genre and you think your friend would love it, too, why not share it with them? Just email or message them a photo of the books instead of lugging them over (and possibly having to lug them back).

If any of the books would be appreciated by a school, you might want to ask school personnel if they're interested. You can also give the books to your local library for their next Friends of the Library sale. Nursing homes always appreciate donated books for their residents. Christian books are often needed by church libraries. Depending on the nature of the books you no longer need, you can surely find somewhere specific to donate them, and use local thrift stores as a backup. Remember, we sentimental types have an easier time giving up belongings if they're going somewhere meaningful.

A few books might actually be worth enough that you can sell them and make some money. Look up titles on Amazon Seller Central to get an idea of what sells these days. Vintage or collectible titles might bring more money at a specialty book store site like Powell's, as will popular books. (If Powell's wants to buy your book, they'll pay the cost of shipping it to them. Go to the Web and type

powells.com/sell-books and input the ISBNs of books you hope to sell to see if they're interested.) If you live near a Half Price Books, you can bring in books to see if they want to buy them.

Of course you can sell your books online at places like Amazon Seller Central. But it may take quite a while before someone finds your listings, and once you finally make a sale, you have to pack and ship it. And of course, you have to store the books in the meantime, which means keeping clutter instead of reducing it.

Another option is **paperbackswap.com**; your books go to someone who wants them and you get credit you can use for books you've been wanting to read (despite the name, hardcover books are included). It's a great solution for bookworms, but it won't reduce your clutter until someone finds and requests the books you're giving up.

So after you've removed the books you're giving away, and any books you might try to sell, you're left with the Keep pile. Do you still have more books than you can comfortably display in your living areas? If your answer is yes, keep going.

First off, which books do you doubt you'll ever read again? They need to go. If you're unsure, try flipping through them to see if your interest is piqued. Some books are so good that we reread them over the years and it's like revisiting an old friend. But most books don't fall into that category.

Persist in reducing your Keep pile, and do *not* decide to keep them all and put them into storage. This is a bad idea: the paper will pick up a musty smell that you'll never be able to get rid of (don't ask me how I know this). Besides, if you're putting books in storage, they clearly aren't essential to your life; why not pass them along so someone else can enjoy them?

If you're very emotionally attached to a book, you can keep the dust jacket and frame it; pass the book along, and when you want to read it again, get it from the library or buy the eBook. (This is a great idea if the book was given to you as a gift, and reminds you of the giver.) You can always put the titles to books you give up but might want to reread someday on your Nook or Kindle wish list. That way, if and when you get the urge to reread it, you can easily buy it. Before you do this, however, make sure you can still get each title in some form. Occasionally, you'll discover that a beloved book is out of print, not at the library (even via Interlibrary Loan), not available in eBook form and ridiculously expensive to buy used. In that case, you're more than justified in keeping the book!

Many people replace most of their books with eBooks, and then give away or sell the books. But some publishers charge far too much for eBooks, sometimes almost as much as the retail price of the physical book. You might not want to pay $10 or $12 for an eBook, especially when many used books are available in thrift stores for a dollar or less. In that case, it's worth keeping the physical book, but only if you truly love it. Again, you may love your books, but you can't keep them all, so you need to decide which ones mean the very most to you.

That's why, as with our other sentimental items, you'll need to rank your books and keep only your favorite few. If you have a huge library, you might try ranking them within categories: your three favorite cookbooks, your five favorite romance novels, etc. The goal is to winnow down your library to your very favorites, the ones you just can't bear to give up. Then store them on shelves in the living areas of your home, where you'll see them regularly and can easily grab one when you feel like reading. Also, a bookshelf full of books in a guest room is a welcoming sight to visiting relatives or friends.

Some of your categories may be books from a particularly happy time in your past. For instance, I had a very large collection of children's books. Even after I encouraged my adult children to take the books that were special to them, far too many remained; I was emotionally attached to most of them because they were an integral part of those long-ago days when my children were young, and I also knew that many of the books were no longer available in public libraries. At the time I downsized, I did not have any grandchildren yet, but I hoped I would eventually get some. So I set aside one small shelf's worth of my favorites, and donated the rest. Now I do have grandchildren, and I read them these books when they visit. For that reason I'm so glad I saved the best books, but I'm also glad I didn't keep *all* of our children's books, because that would have taken up far too much space in my little house.

As you go through your books, you may find some that you never read. Often, such a book represents who you were at one time. The fact that you never bothered to read it indicates that it's not really interesting to you anymore (unless you completely forgot that you had this title and you intend to read it very, very soon). I found books I had always intended to read but never did. When we downsized, I kept those that still interested me, read them over time and then donated them when I was done with them. I don't think I kept a single one. But after I found them, I enjoyed the anticipation of knowing I had books to be read waiting for me.

Another category I reduced greatly was cookbooks. I had many, but most only had one or two recipes in them that I used regularly. So I copied the recipes and got rid of most of the cookbooks; I only kept seven of them. I have a file of those recipe copies that I refer to regularly, and it takes up far less space than all those cookbooks did.

Sometimes books are part of a series that you once collected, and maybe still do. It's so hard to break up a collection, but unless there's any chance that you will reread the series all the way through (be honest with yourself), it's OK to get rid of the whole collection, or just keep a couple of your very favorites and give up the rest. I kept my entire Rex Stout mystery collection, and I still reread those books from time to time. I never get tired of them.

As for my Nancy Drews? Having kept them for so many years, I dreaded letting them go, but I finally admitted to myself that I was no longer interested in reading them. One of my daughters once told me she would take any Nancy Drews that I might give up. So I kept three: two of the original three that my aunt gave me, and one whose cover reminds me that I reread it more times than any of the others. Those three now sit on the bookshelf in my office. The rest of the Nancy Drews belong to my daughter now.

Remember, if you're successful and can get rid of the bulk of your books, you'll still have your very favorites, plus there's always the public library, where there are more books than you could ever read in a lifetime, and none of them are filling up your house! Also, your bookshelves will look much better if they hold a mix of beloved books and a few decorative items with space around them rather than books packed in tight from left to right, and sideways at the top of each shelf to boot.

You may even find that you're secretly relieved to be rid of most of your books. That's how Ardis felt: a contractor told her that her dining room ceiling was starting to fall apart because she had far too many boxes stored above it in her attic. She asked her grandsons to bring down the boxes, and was horrified to discover that she had nearly 80 boxes full of books up there. The boys helped her go through them; she kept only a few dozen books and donated the rest to the library at her local hospital, where she'd borrowed books to read while having chemotherapy a few years earlier. Now her books offer a respite to others going through treatment; meanwhile, she's very glad that her newly patched-up dining room ceiling should stay where it belongs.

Once you've reduced your personal library to just your very best books, you'll need to be vigilant so that your house doesn't start looking like a bookstore again (we bookworms tend to attract more books, you know!) Consider adopting a policy of "one book in, one book out." By only allowing yourself to buy another book if you give up one you already own, you'll keep your library from taking over your house while reaffirming your opinion of which books are your most precious books.

Babies' and Kids' Clothes, Toys, Artwork and Schoolwork

Anyone with any sentimental genes at all who happens to be a parent struggles with giving up their children's clothes and toys, and I totally understand why.

I was very attached to my kids' clothes, especially the tiny outfits they wore during that all-too-brief first year. I saved boxes and boxes of my favorite little clothes and toys, despite having given up many less-loved items during previous small purges. Even though I have plenty of photos of my children when they were young, holding their little duds always brought back cherished memories.

Keeping baby clothes made sense while I was having more children; using each child's hand-me-downs for the next child saved us a small fortune. But when we were forced to downsize, my kids were in their teens and 20s. There was no need for me to still have so many baby clothes and toys stored away. But I had never been able to give them up.

However, desperate times call for desperate measures. We moved three times in four years, getting rid of lots of stuff each time. The baby clothes went very early in the process, and I only allowed myself to keep two boxes that also included several crocheted baby afghans made by our grandmothers for our children. Everything else went to Goodwill.

It helped knowing that there are young families who need affordable secondhand baby clothes; the clothes I had saved were in good shape so I knew they would be useful.

That's why Goodwill was a much better choice than just throwing all those little outfits in a dumpster. But if I'd had the time, I would have preferred to donate them to a fund-raising sale for a group that helps children, here or overseas.

As for the clothes I kept, I thought maybe future grandchildren could wear them. I've since discovered that new parents want new clothes for their offspring, and they get more than they need thanks to generous friends and relatives, not to mention the torrent of gifts from baby showers.

So those few outfits I kept still sit in a box that I go through from time to time. Since I saved my kids' coming-home outfits, my grandson did get to wear the outfit that his dad came home from the hospital in, though not when he himself came home from the hospital. For that event, he wore a very 21st century tuxedo onesie.

I'm also glad I kept those afghans. My daughter went through the box and took a few home with her shortly before she had her first child. That little one is now a toddler who has adopted one of the afghans. It tickles me every time I see her drag her "blankie" around, knowing it was made by her great, great-grandmother.

Clothes Overload

When I was raising children, we had plenty of clothes for them. But today's parents have more than plenty, it seems. Recently I went to a garage sale to find a few goodies for a new granddaughter who will be arriving soon. The sale was held in a two-car garage that was filled with tables overflowing with girls' clothes ranging from newborn size to size 7.

Each table held a different size, and was heaped up with stacks of clothes. I asked the lady holding the garage sale how many daughters she had, and was shocked when she said just one.

No wonder that some of the outfits still had tags on them. How many different outfits can one child possibly wear before outgrowing that size? After all, most children grow like weeds in the early years.

Perhaps you've also been blessed with generous people in your life, and are awash in baby clothes, toddler clothes, and kid clothes to the point that you're running out of room for them. But every time you try to get rid of them, you picture your little angel in them. Even the outfits that were never worn may be hard to give up because the giver is or was someone important in your life.

Then there's the possibility that you may have another child at some point and will need the clothes. That's a handy excuse for keeping everything instead of making the tough decisions now.

Do yourself a favor and be selective *now*. If you think there might be another child coming down the road, keep one box of really good, unstained, classic-looking baby clothes (especially sleepers and onesies) just in case. Unisex is a plus. Then make decisions about the rest. I'll show you how shortly.

Ouch! This Hurts!

Your children's first years were so precious, and they went so fast. Even on days when your little darling has gotten on your last nerve, all you have to do is remember them as a baby and you melt like butter.

But you can't bring back those years by keeping all those little clothes. Yes, they do trigger memories, but there are ways you can keep those memories without keeping every little outfit (not to mention every bib, sock, onesie and hat.)

However, before you can give up any of these beloved items, you'll have to remind yourself (as often as necessary) that:

- You've made the decision to live with less clutter,

- You're tired of all these clothes taking up so much physical space that you could use for other things,

- You're tired of all these clothes taking up so much mental space, weighing on your mind and clogging up your mental to-do list, and

- You can't bring those lovely early days of your child's existence back by keeping every little thing they ever wore.

That said, you don't have to get rid of *all* the clothes. It's OK to keep a few precious little duds. In a bit, you'll learn some ways to do that. But keep in mind that the more you get rid of, the more open space you'll have in your home and in your storage areas. And that feels *so good*.

So, step 1 is to go through all of your stored baby and toddler clothes and sort them into piles. How do you decide what goes into which pile? Here are the rules:

Pile 1 is for the items that aren't in good shape. The fronts are full of formula or food stains. They're missing snaps. They're faded, or something else in the wash bled on them and now they have random stains. Perhaps they look fine, but when you stretch out the waist of the pants or the top of the sock, the dried elastic hisses and the item becomes very stretched out. Time for them to go!

Pile 2 is for the items that aren't your favorites but are in pretty good shape: the onesies, the socks, the pastel-colored sleepers that still have all their snaps, the bibs that never got used because they had a silly message or represented the wrong football team.

Pile 3 is for items that don't really bring back memories but are in great shape, or still have the tags on, including designer baby clothes. These are the things that you can give up if you really have to, but you don't want to because they're so nice.

Pile 4 is for anything precious, anything very memorable, anything that's a gift from someone you love, that you just hate to give up. This includes the coming home outfit, the first Christmas outfit, and the knitted infant cardigan that was never used but was made by your favorite aunt who has since passed away. Depending on how sentimental you are, this may become your largest pile, or stack, or mountain.

Good places to do this sorting include your bed, your kitchen table or even the living room sofa. Anywhere that's inconvenient to have stuff scattered all over on is good; that will force you to finish this task soon so you can sleep, eat or watch television again. (When my children were younger, I once went through ALL of their outgrown clothes by bringing them down to the living room and sorting them on the floor. I had piles of boys' and girls' clothes in sizes from newborn to preteen stretching the 26-foot length of our living room. It took me days to go through everything because I kept getting bogged down or distracted; to make matters worse, I wasn't forced to finish the task right away because we rarely used the living room. What a decluttering nightmare!)

Keep at this task until you're finished. As you go along, you may have second thoughts about what goes in which pile. That's fine unless everything seems to be going into pile 4. Then you'll need to give yourself a few quick pep talks, reminding yourself how nice it will feel to have the extra space once you've gone through all these things and moved them on.

Remember, the goal is not to get rid of every trace of your children's infancy and childhood. But there's no need to keep *everything*, even if you hope to have more children.

What to Do with Pile 1

Now that you're done sorting, let's start with the easiest pile first. As you may have guessed, this is the Pitch pile. (I didn't want to call it that right away because it's too hard to think of pitching these things right from the start.) The items in Pile 1 have outlived their usefulness. They're stained, they're ripped, they're faded; bottom line, they don't look so good. Please don't donate these items as you'll just make more work for someone else to cull them out, because no one wants to put their little one into ugly, stained clothes. Just pitch them without a bit of guilt, but with gratitude that they served your family well... and do it right away.

Now doesn't that feel good?

What to Do with Pile 2

The items in Pile 2 are useful and easy to give up, so they're the items you'll donate. If you know of a rummage sale or thrift shop that's connected to one of your favorite charities, that's the place to donate them. If you're planning on selling your excess baby and kids' clothes, these will help bulk up your garage sale, or you can try selling them in groups on **Facebook.com** or **craigslist.org** with a headline similar to this: "24 baby boy items, size newborn-12 months, $20 or best offer." Be sure to include a couple of sharp photos of the items as a group.

What to Do with Pile 3

If you're planning to have a garage sale, the items in Pile 3 will be your best items, the ones you want to display prominently on your tables and photograph for any online ads you might create. People love buying items with the tags left on, and you can ask more money for them, too. If some items are designer brands, try selling them individually online if they don't sell at the garage sale. Whatever doesn't sell can be donated to your favorite charity; those items should be good sellers for them, so you'll really be helping them out.

What to Do with Pile 4

If this pile is a mountain, you've got to pare it down. This isn't easy, but as we've done with other items, you'll need to categorize and prioritize. If you have more than one child, divide the items into groups by child. You may decide to keep the coming home outfits, like I did, or the baptism outfits, or their first shoes. We all have our preferences. The goal is to winnow down the keepers to just a few for each child.

Most likely, this means that some precious items will have to go. After her divorce, Molly moved to a small apartment with very little storage space, and had to give up many of her boxes filled with items from the past. Her daughter's baptism gown was one of those things that she just didn't have room for. It was an expensive smocked Polly Flinders gown from the 1980s, and it was gorgeous. She ended up selling it on **eBay.com** for the asking price, but took no joy in the sale until she got an email from the buyer, who told her that she was thrilled with her purchase for her new baby girl, and that the gown was extra special because those gowns aren't made anymore. The buyer's joy eased Molly's pain, and she could still "see" the gown whenever she wished because she had taken photographs of it for the eBay ad.

Keep in mind that even if you keep every one of the items in Pile 4, they will slowly rot away. They won't do anyone any good, and you won't look at them and enjoy the memories they help bring back because you can't see them buried in boxes in your attic or basement. Doesn't it make more sense to keep just a few of your very favorite items, and send the rest where they'll help someone else?

Here are a few things you can do with those extra-precious items, the cream of the crop of Pile 4, so that you can see them while also enjoying more open space in your home:

- Arrange an outfit, a favorite baby toy, a lock of hair and the hospital bracelet in a shadow box and hang it on the wall or display it on a table.

- Make (or have someone else make) a baby clothes quilt from your child's outgrown outfits to hang on a wall. (Find ideas for how to do this on **Pinterest.com.**)

- Put one tiny sweater or sleeper on a doll or teddy bear and keep it on a bed or chair.

- Have a very special garment, such as a christening gown or outfit, heirloomed by a good dry cleaner so it's ready for a future grandchild.

- Keep a clear plastic box of the very best outfits in an upstairs (not basement) closet, where it's readily accessible so you can give such items to a younger child or grandchild.

When my son was three or four, his most beloved piece of clothing was his "Ernie coat," a yellow plastic raincoat with a giant picture of Ernie from "Sesame Street" on the back. How he loved that coat! It made the cut of most precious baby clothes when we downsized. My son is now 6'4", but he has a little son who also enjoys "Sesame Street." Recently my son's wife sent us a photo of our grandson wearing the Ernie coat that I saved. As you can imagine, I just love that photo. And I don't need the Ernie coat back when my grandson outgrows it. It has served its purpose, as far as I'm concerned.

Of course, my son didn't want any of his clothes that I'd kept, and didn't even know I had the raincoat. I kept that because *I* wanted it. I've found that most adult offspring (especially men) really don't care about clothes from their childhood, so if you're keeping baby clothes because you think your kids will want them someday, you're probably wasting your time (and space). That said, keeping some for yourself if you have room and will actually look at them again is a different story. Yvette has just one son; he was the only child she was able to have. She kept a lot of his baby clothes and toys as well as her maternity clothes, and regularly went through them to relive the memories. Years later, she decided she didn't need all those clothes around. So she cut them into squares and made a quilt out of them that now hangs on a rocking chair in her home. She only has a few other small items from his infancy that she keeps in a decorative box on a shelf, and she is content.

Older Kids' Clothes

It's much easier to get rid of your children's clothes as they get older. They grow so fast, and the outgrown clothes pile up, but most of the clothes don't seem to rev up our sentimental feelings the way baby and toddler clothes do.

Most kids don't become that attached to their old clothes, especially since they get to replace them with new clothes. So the best thing to do is to make room for the new clothes and move the old clothes on as soon as you can.

Often the child (or teen) isn't interested in keeping any of those clothes around, but a sentimental parent wants to do so. Vicki had this problem. Her son Henry could not have cared less what happened to his old clothes; he just didn't want to deal with them. One August, she forced him to put down the video game controller and go through all of his clothes before school began, making him try on things so she could determine what no longer fit and therefore what she needed to buy for him. They succeeded in making lots of room in his closet, and a huge pile of outgrown clothes on his bed that she intended to take to their church's rummage sale. Then her husband Brian came home and caught sight of the clothes. He couldn't believe Vicki would give up all of

Henry's old clothes, and suggested they put them in the attic instead.

After all the work she and Henry had done, Vicki had no desire to keep the clothes in the attic or anywhere else in the house. In fact, she was tempted to wait until Brian was gone and run them over to church for the sale. But she knew that wouldn't be right. Instead, after a long marital discussion, she and Brian went through the clothes and he picked out a few items to put away in one box in the attic; then she was able to donate the rest.

Toys

Going through your children's toys is more challenging than going through their clothes, because they're probably a lot more interested in keeping their toys than their clothes. But toys are outgrown just as clothes are, and kids are always interested in getting new toys, so encourage them to make room for the new by giving up the old. If you can get them to participate in finding toys they're too old to play with, or toys they are no longer interested in, you can have them come with you when you give them to a younger friend or to a charity, so that they see that it's good to help others by sharing items that you have loved but no longer need.

Given my childhood experience with my mother the clean-sweeper, I vowed that I would never get rid of my kids' most beloved toys behind their backs. This meant I had to work *with* them to make decisions about what to give up. I learned that it's best to have some kind of visual limit for them, like a number limit on certain types of toys, or a size limit, such as "you can keep whatever you can fit in the toy box." This taught them to make choices; a toy box overflowing with too many toys was the reason for the purge in the first place.

I never let my kids have full access to all of their toys, either. Just before Christmas or birthdays, I'd take some of their toys, box them up and hide them in the basement. Once the big day arrived, they had lots of new toys to play with, and forgot about their other toys. A few months later, when all the Christmas or birthday toys had lost their novelty, I'd bring out the boxed toys and it was as though *they* were brand new again. While the kids greeted those toys with shrieks of joy, I boxed up and hid the new toys that had become old hat. This was a cycle I repeated for years; I often brought a box of toys out of storage on a day when I had some chore I wanted to get done and didn't want to be interrupted. Those "new" toys kept the kids busy for hours.

(I will admit that sometimes when I went to get the box of toys out of storage, I might notice one or two annoyingly noisy toys and set them aside for donation. I don't think any of the kids ever realized that, but I figured if something had been boxed away for months and they hadn't even asked about it, donating it wouldn't hurt them.)

If your kids are grown and their toys haven't been played with for years, the cardinal rule is: don't keep toys for adult children when they haven't expressed an interest in keeping them. Your kids may not be as sentimental as you are, and won't appreciate being loaded down with boxes of old toys when they leave home someday. If there are toys they really want to keep, they'll tell you.

Years ago, kids had fewer toys and became more attached to those they had. Unlike today's kids, we didn't have movies or video games, so toys were more precious to us. Today's kids have so many toys that they might not care if you regularly reduce the load, but you might find yourself attached to some of the toys they once loved. There's no point keeping them unless they're of particularly high quality and you want to put them away for your grandchildren someday. But before doing so, consider how your children would feel about the toys *you* played with. Each generation is different from the one before. I saved some of my cherished Barbie doll clothes and let my daughters use them for their dolls, but they always preferred new Barbie clothes in the latest styles. My husband kept a box of his beloved Matchbox cars but our sons never seemed too interested in them. So even if you keep some toys, they might not be played with again. Why not give them to others who will play with them now?

If you absolutely must keep a few of your children's old toys as mementos, think about how you can display them. Dennis kept a small collection of his children's baby toys and a few of his own. He put them in a little red wagon, covered it with a piece of glass, and it became a small table/conversation piece in his office. Arthur, who is a great-grandfather, has had a small fishbowl full of marbles that he played with as a child on display in his living room for many years.

Many of today's toys are licensed characters from current television shows or movies. Today's popular characters will mean nothing to your grandchildren someday, and they'll only be worth something to the collectors of the future if they're still in the original packaging, which probably didn't happen if your children actually played with them. (The same goes for all the tiny pieces for character-related houses and vehicles.)

Sometimes it's the most mundane toys that get kids' attention. When my children were young, my mother-in-law found some random stuffed animals in her attic and put them in her spare room, along with a small kids' desk and an old toy stroller. When we'd come to visit, my kids made a beeline for that room. As they got older, Grandma started saving her junk mail in a pile on the little desk, and the kids would play office and write on all the forms and envelopes. They had great fun doing that; go figure! So even if you don't save many or any toys, you'll find a way to entertain your future grandchildren when they come over.

Try to find families with younger children who can use your children's old toys, because you may not be able to donate all of the toys to charities. Some health departments have instituted stricter rules about used toys, so many thrift stores no longer accept them. (At the time of this writing, Goodwill still takes them.) However, non-profit organizations that work with kids are often interested in them, as are churches that have nurseries. Charities that work with foster children and families in crisis are often looking for nice toys, so please don't donate anything that's broken or is missing pieces. Just throw them out.

If you suspect an old toy is a collectible item, research the "sold" section on **eBay.com** to see if it actually does have value. If so, sell it. If not, move it along.

Finally, for those toys you want to keep, whether they belong to your children or to you, consider what they're made of. Plastic holds up for years, but fabric and paper rot. Any toy that takes batteries is useless without them, and the batteries they use may not be available in the future. Be very picky about what you keep; take photos of the most cherished toys if you wish, and then give away or sell the vast majority of them.

Artwork and Schoolwork

Your child's artwork and schoolwork is so precious. Everything they create shows how they're growing and learning. How can you give up a single piece of it?

I couldn't. I had boxes and boxes of work done by each of my children. We're talking literally thousands of pieces of paper, stuffed in plastic and cardboard boxes that were stacked in my basement. When it came time to move, all of those boxes went to storage, where they waited until I could get to them. As I began to go through them, saving the best, preparing to pitch the rest, and brushing tiny little bugs off many of them, I realized that this just was not going to work. I had no room for all of these things, and my now-grown kids not only didn't want any of it, they thought it was ridiculous that I kept so much of it. (I homeschooled them, so I kept a lot of it in case I ever needed to show the authorities proof of what they'd been learning. Do this year after year for each child, and you end up with *a lot* of paper!) In the end, I found a couple of really nice pieces of artwork or stories by each child, then put the rest in the recycler without going through it piece by piece and page by page. I'm talking about artwork, workbooks, construction paper creations, reports, the whole nine yards. The few things I kept went into the single box I kept for each child.

This was very painful at the time, but now it doesn't bother me. I finally realized that my kids are the proof of their education. They've all turned out great. It doesn't matter which one wrote the adorable book about butterflies and which one made a basketball poster that looks like it was done by a much older kid. I don't need those original artifacts as proof of my kids' abilities...my kids are the proof.

Nevertheless, I understand how proud we parents are of our children and why we want to keep these things. But we can't; most of us don't have room, and even if we do have room, paper rots and attracts those tiny little bugs (and worse), and let's face it, we're never going to go through all those boxes of stored artwork and schoolwork anyways.

As we've done with our other precious things, if you must keep some of it, go through and find the very best items, the ones you especially love, and pitch the rest. Only keep the best if you're going to put it on display or keep it where you can see it regularly. This is where taking photos and making books comes in. You can take photos of each child's best items and put them into a book (**Shutterfly.com** does nice work) or just keep them on your computer. Better yet, take photos of your child with the item they made and put *those* photos in a book or keep them in your computer.

Don't throw out artwork if it was done recently; that could really hurt your child's feelings. Put it away for a while and then pitch it when they're not around. Drawings or paintings that are especially important to them can be displayed in their bedrooms; they'll replace them as they make new ones.

If your kids are still at home and you can't make yourself do this yet, you may have to wait until they're a bit older, or until you really need that extra storage space and are sufficiently motivated to pitch, pitch, pitch. I've heard of people who laboriously scan their children's preschool artwork and put them in frames that fill entire walls in their homes. To be honest, that sounds a little obsessive to me, and might create some tiny egotists in the process. If you can save a few things and let go of the rest now, you'll thank yourself someday.

This goes double for artwork and school projects that are three-dimensional. You don't have room for these! Take a photo and then send them to the trash can. The value is not in the item itself, but in what your child learned by creating it, and in the memories made when they did it.

Sometimes your kids make precious little things for you that you hate to give up. When we packed up to move out of our family home, I kept finding little rocks that the kids had saved for me. Some were "special" rocks they had found, and others were rocks they had hand-painted for me. By the time I found them, I couldn't remember who had given me which rock, so I just put them all in the garden of my new home without any guilt.

If you have a hard time giving up your children's artwork and other schoolwork, consider this: if you keep it all, someday when your children have to go through your estate, how will they feel about finding box after box of old yellowed papers teeming with bugs and mold? I'm guessing they won't be touched by your sentimentality.

The Truth About Your Children's Belongings

Whether we're talking about giving up baby clothes, toys, artwork or schoolwork, the issue is not mere sentimentality. It's about letting go of our children. Letting go of them is hard, and it hurts, but it's necessary if our kids are going to become independent adults. As they fly away from us, pursuing new adventures without us, the little things they leave behind seem just too precious to give up. We think that keeping all of those things will let us keep a little of each child who left us.

Of course, nothing could be further from the truth. Our children have grown up and moved on. This is how it's supposed to be. We were never supposed to keep them in the first place. All the wonderful memories we made with them led up to the moment we had to let them go; keeping so much tangible evidence of those memories may temporarily assuage the pain, but it won't change anything.

If we keep all those things, we postpone our acceptance of the situation. We also postpone *our* new life, the one where we get to do the things *we* want to do now that we have the time and the space. The time gets eaten up when we stack and rearrange boxes full of our kids' stuff, trying to make a little more room. That's what eats up the space, too. We may fool ourselves by saying that we're saving these things for our kids because they might want them someday, but the reality is that if your adult child comes home and just sits around going through their childhood belongings, something has gone wrong in their life. Most people are too busy living their lives to go digging through their past, unless they're really unhappy. You don't want that to happen, do you?

No, you're keeping all this evidence of their childhood because you're trying to hold on to them for a little longer. But you can't: they're gone. You'll always have your good memories, whether or not you keep their stuff. So ask your children if they want any of their childhood things. If they do, that's great. Let them take it all and don't ask them what they did with it. But if they don't want any of it (and they probably don't), take a few photos if you need to, keep just a few precious items where you can see them regularly (if you need to), then get rid of the rest and move on to the exciting new stage of your life: the one where you have more time and space to do as you wish.

You don't want to be like Betty. She saved boxes and boxes of her three daughters' lovely outgrown dresses, petticoats, dress coats and patent leather shoes for her future granddaughters. Her attic was filled with these boxes. At one point she wanted to turn the attic into an art studio so she could take up watercolor painting, a lifelong dream. But she never went through with it because she had nowhere else to store all those beautiful clothes. As it turned out, two of her daughters never married or had children, and the third had five boys. Now Betty can no longer make it up the attic steps, and those clothes sit in those boxes, growing more musty and moth-chewed by the year. Back in the 1950s and 1960s, other little girls would have loved being given such nice things, but after Betty dies, these items will all be thrown in the trash because they're ruined now.

Possessions of Late Loved Ones, Heirlooms, and Inherited Belongings

When Anita lost her mom, she found that going through her mom's estate was actually comforting for her. That was a good thing, because she had to clear out her mother's apartment right after the funeral. There were only a few weeks left on the lease, so she didn't have the luxury of waiting to go through everything until she was emotionally ready.

Since Anita lived in Montana and her mom had lived in Ohio, she was unable to take many of her mother's belongings with her. So after setting aside a few particularly special pieces of jewelry and some small knick-knacks for herself, and mailing a large box of her mother's personal papers to her home in Montana, she invited her mother's elderly friends over to take any clothing or jewelry they might like. The next morning, she called an estate agent to look at the remaining items (furniture, décor, linens, etc.) and make her an offer on the entire contents of the apartment.

Daisy, the estate agent, was a perky old gal who was kind and supportive to Anita in her grief. Anita warmed to her quickly.

Daisy slowly walked around the living room, taking notes, before checking out the bedroom. She reappeared a few minutes later.

"That chest?" she asked. "The maple one?"

"My mom's hope chest," Anita replied. "My dad made it for her when they got engaged."

"Are you taking it with you?"

"No," Anita said sadly. "I would love to, but there's no room in my house, and besides, I don't know how I'd get it home."

"Well, it's lovely, beautifully made. But the quilts in it aren't old enough to have any real value," Daisy said.

"Quilts? What quilts?"

Realizing she'd forgotten to look inside the hope chest, Anita made a beeline for the bedroom and lifted the heavy lid of the hope chest. Inside she found three like-new quilts, each hand-stitched and made of bright fabric shapes with pastel backgrounds.

"I remember these! Mom always wanted to 'keep them nice,' but sometimes when I was a child we'd take them out and she'd show me where the patches came from. I think this one was made from her childhood dresses....this one has darker colors so it might be from when she was older....oh, and this one was made from *my* clothes when I was little. I recognize the fabrics," Anita said excitedly. "Yes, these are coming with me."

After Anita arrived home, she put two of the quilts in the already overcrowded linen closet, but the quilt from her childhood went on the guest bedroom bed, where her granddaughter slept when she stayed over. Anita loved seeing little Bella asleep under that quilt.

Some time later, when Anita was going through a decluttering phase, she was busy purging the linen closet of faded and frayed towels and washcloths when she looked up at the top shelf and saw her mother's quilts. A wave of guilt washed over her to see them way up there, completely forgotten.

She pulled them out, unfolded them and admired them. That's what she was doing when Matt and Tiffany arrived with Bella.

"Whoa!" Matt said. "Where'd you get those?"

"They were your grandma's," Anita replied. "Would you like them?"

Matt looked at Tiffany, and they exchanged one of those "couple glances."

"Thanks, Mom, but I don't think we need more bed stuff, do we, Tiff?"

Tiffany shook her head, adding, "But thanks anyways, Anita."

"Not for Bella?" Anita asked hopefully.

"She already has that sweet Dora comforter set you gave her, remember?" Tiffany replied.

"Dora! Dora!" Bella sang out as she began dancing around the three of them.

So Anita pushed the quilts back up into the top of the linen closet and went off to play with Bella, figuring she'd think about the quilts some other time.

About a week later, Tiffany's mother Chris called Anita. She said Tiffany had told her about the quilts, and she wondered if Anita would be interested in donating them to a quilt museum in Billings that she had recently visited.

"I don't think the quilt museum would want them, Chris," Anita said. "The estate agent back in Cincinnati looked at them and said they weren't worth much."

"Maybe not worth much in cash," Chris replied. "But in historic value? You never know. The quilt museum's appraiser could tell you. Should I have her call you?"

"Oh...alright," Anita said. "Let's see what she has to say."

The quilt appraiser, Libby, arrived a few days later and couldn't say enough good things about Anita's mom's quilts. She told Anita that they were excellent examples of their time period, and in perfect condition.

"So many people didn't appreciate what went into quilts," Libby explained. "To them, quilts were something that went on a bed and later, when they began to show wear, were wrapped around furniture in the back of a truck when they moved. That's why it's rare to find handmade quilts like these in such pristine condition. They're just lovely! If you would consider donating them to the museum, we would be so grateful, and they would both have placards nearby with your mother's name and some other information on them."

Anita caught her breath. It never occurred to her that her mom's simple quilts might go into a museum. She suddenly had a vision of taking a teenaged Bella to the museum to see her great-grandmother's quilts on display. Then tears filled her eyes.

"Yes, Libby," Anita said. "I think that's the perfect place for them. Mom would be so proud, and I am, too."

Anita's decision honored her mother's memory and let her give up the quilts without pain. There's nothing wrong with giving up heirlooms or other family belongings that you treasure but can't use, especially when you find a way to honor those items and the memories they represent by sending them somewhere meaningful. This is the key to giving up items you've never thought you could part with: they have to go somewhere special, not just into a donation box. The destination of each item is very important; you'll feel much better if you know those things are helping or providing enjoyment to others.

Choosing a special place for special belongings is how sentimental people successfully declutter while minimizing emotional pain. There are historical groups that would love your Dad's uniform from his service during the Vietnam War, or your grandmother's collection of Adlai Stevenson campaign buttons. Your late loved one's belongings aren't doing anyone any good in the back of your closet, and besides, you need the closet space for other things, right?

Let a Little Time (Not Decades) Pass Before You Go Through Everything

Grieving takes time, so if your loss is very recent, you may not be able to give up things quickly unless you're forced to, as Anita was. Be warned, however, that if there's no deadline (such as a lease expiration or an impending house sale) forcing you to go through everything, it will be very easy to either leave it all where it is or to store it all in your home or storage unit. That will work for a while, but sooner or later, you'll have to deal with your loved one's belongings.

The possessions late loved ones leave behind might be the most emotionally challenging category of the Sentimental Seven. We may feel that those items are all we have left of our loved one, so we can't imagine giving them up.

That said, everyone handles grief in their own way, which explains why one man will purge the house of every item that belonged to his recently deceased wife because they're all such painful reminders of what he's lost, while another man will leave his house exactly as it was the day his wife died, and it will stay that way for years. You can't put a timetable on grief; getting through the loss of a loved one takes as long as it takes. But sometimes life forces us to go through our late loved one's belongings whether or not we feel ready, because of outside circumstances.

If your loss occurred many years ago, and you never went through any of your inherited belongings, consider what has been keeping you from doing so. It could be that you're overwhelmed by the task, or that lethargy keeps you from even considering it. Is it possible you'd rather not deal with it and are actually counting on *your* heirs to go through it for you someday? That may be what was going on with Edna and Henry, a story I shared in *Downsizing Your Life for Freedom, Flexibility and Financial Peace:*

> Sometimes parents or other relatives pass down items to us that have been in our family for years. We don't want to be the ones who let go of such "valuable heirlooms." And so they sit, untouched, practically invisible, yet they're in our way and they keep us from moving on. Occasionally, being "keeper of the heirlooms" becomes even more important than the heirlooms themselves.

> That was the case with Edna and Henry. Thirty years ago, they lost their mothers a few months apart and inherited many of their belongings, which they stashed in every nook and cranny of their house. They never used them; they didn't need to. But the couple didn't feel right about

getting rid of their mothers' things, so there they sat, for years.

One day a friend from church called, asking if they had a sewing machine she could borrow to make patchwork quilts for charity as part of a church project. Edna refused the request, saying that while they did have their mothers' sewing machines stored in a closet, she didn't want them to be accidentally broken. Edna's friend pointed out that using an old machine actually helps keep it in good working order, because sitting unused is very bad for sewing machines (the plastic and rubber parts dry up due to lack of maintenance).

But Edna stood her ground. Today, twenty years later, those sewing machines still sit in that closet. They're probably unusable by now. Someone will have to throw them away after Edna and Henry pass on.

Don't do that to your heirs. If it's been a long time since you went through items you inherited, try again. You might be surprised at how the passage of time enables you to let go of several or maybe even most of the inherited items you've been avoiding for years.

If your loss is more recent, please know that as you heal over time, the prospect of going through all those belongings will become less daunting. Once you can consider the possibility of doing so without falling apart emotionally, start making plans for a decluttering session. Think about whether you'd prefer to do it alone, or if you need some help. Relatives or friends who are also grieving your loved one may benefit by helping you go through everything. Remember, you don't have to do it all at once. Letting things go in stages might be the best way to perform this task.

Occasionally people become overwhelmed by the thought of doing this and just pack up everything and donate it all at once so they don't have to think about it any more. Try not to give in if you get this impulse; you might really regret it later. It can actually be therapeutic to make the thoughtful-but-tough decisions about your loved one's belongings, and you may actually feel a bit better after doing so.

Heirloom Furniture

Out of the Sentimental Seven, heirlooms and inherited possessions tend to include the largest items: furniture. People often inherit an entire household, including beds, sofas, dining sets and the like. Most people don't have the room to store extra furniture; paying for storage for big items could tax anyone's piggy bank. But if a given piece of furniture is something that was passed down from a previous generation, it's probably already considered an heirloom in your family, and you'll likely feel guilty getting rid of it.

Look at inherited furniture on an individual basis. Consider that today's new furniture isn't nearly as well-made as furniture used to be. Is it possible that you can replace some of your own furniture with the furniture you inherited, thus keeping a family heirloom and improving your own situation at the same time? In our household, we use (on a daily basis) my grandmother's maple dresser, my great-uncle's solid walnut nightstand, and the headboard, foot board and bed frame my husband slept in as a child (it has a new mattress and box spring on it).

If the inherited furniture has a classic look, it can mix with a variety of decorating styles.

If a piece of furniture holds good memories for you, you'll love seeing it every day in your home.

If you like a piece but it doesn't fit in with your style, go to **Pinterest.com** and see how people creatively recycle old furniture these days. I just saw a 1990s entertainment center that someone turned into a very cool play kitchen for their children. I never would have guessed that play kitchen's origins if I hadn't seen the "Before" photos.

For items that just won't fit into your home, consider other members of your family who may be interested in them. Take photos and email or text them to your relatives. Perhaps a young relative setting up their first apartment might be interested. Try to keep furniture in the family; if that doesn't work out, at least you'll know you tried.

Clothes

Going through a late loved one's clothes can be very challenging, especially if you had a close relationship. It can be hard to part with the memories triggered by the clothes your loved one wore. If you both wore the same size, you might want to keep a few things for yourself; there's nothing wrong with that. Even if you weren't the same size, certain pieces of clothing might have great meaning for you. Kenny kept his mom's cardigan where he could easily see it and hug it; he said it still smelled like his mom and comforted him. Danuta had her mom's best Sunday dress altered to fit her and wears it whenever she needs a lift.

As we discussed in the last chapter, clothes that hold sentimental value for you can be restyled into quilts or pillows so that you have a tangible reminder of your loved one in your home where you can see it, touch it and enjoy it on a daily basis. Sharon had her late husband's t-shirts (from marathons he ran) made into a quilt that now hangs on the wall of her den.

Wedding gowns are often passed down in families. Offer them to anyone in the family who is planning to get married and sees the value of wearing something that belonged to an ancestor. If there are no takers, but you'd like to keep something for future generations, cut out a small piece of the gown and label it. In years to come, when there is a bride in your family, she can pin that keepsake in her own gown as "something old." You can also donate old wedding gowns to community theater companies, or high schools for their drama classes. As long as you have a wedding photo of your late loved one, you don't need the actual gown, too.

Diaries and Personal Letters

If you should inherit a loved one's personal papers, please go through them with care. It's possible your loved one's memories are there in the form of diaries, journals and personal correspondence. These are part of a family's history, and don't usually take up so much space that they're a burden. (You can scan them and keep them in your computer, if you're short on space for the actual letters. This will also preserve them.)

If they are something you believe extended family members would be interested in, you can make a blog with them. That's what Brenda did. Her elderly father Leonard got a call from a couple rehabbing a house they bought, who found about 70 letters hidden under a floorboard in their attic. Using the Internet, they researched the names in the letters by calling people in the area and asking if they recognized the names. That's how they found Leonard, and they gave him the letters.

It turned out that the letters, now faded and very fragile, were written by Leonard's mother to her mother during the 1920s and 1930s (the couple's house once belonged to Leonard's grandmother). Leonard wanted the rest of the family to be able to read the letters but worried that they would fall apart as they were passed around. He wasn't sure what to do until Brenda suggested scanning the letters to preserve them.

So Brenda and her family scanned the letters and began posting them to a blog. Then they notified their relatives of the existence of the blog; family members can now subscribe to the blog and read their ancestor's letters as they are posted.

If you're not interested in keeping inherited journals or correspondence, find a family member who is. If no one in the family wants them, and they appear to be of historic value, consider donating them to a historical society museum.

Guilt

Sometimes people feel guilty for getting rid of their loved one's belongings. This is especially true if the loved one used to say things like, "Don't ever sell my coin collection!" or "I built this house with my own hands and it better stay in the family after I'm gone." Often these things were said decades ago, but they reverberate through the years and might make you feel guilty when you remember them. Most people, however, would not want to leave burdens behind for their loved ones to deal with after they're gone, and would certainly not want them to feel guilty about getting rid of their belongings.

After someone passes away, those who inherit their belongings can do whatever they wish with them. That's just a fact of life. But if you loved the person, you'll go through their estate with thought and care. Items that you know for a fact were very important to them should go to a good home, even if it isn't yours. As for the less-special items, which probably make up the bulk of their estate, send them where they can do the most good. That's a great way to honor someone's memory.

Also, if you feel guilty or sad about giving up belongings of a loved one that didn't make the cut of your top three or top ten, and no one else in your family wants them, consider selling them for whatever you can get for them and donating the proceeds to a cause that was important to your loved one, or to you. We often feel we must get top dollar for such items, but the fact is that antiques and mementos are a much harder sell than they used to be. If you can turn them into money for a good cause, you'll feel much better than if you sell them for pennies, or worse, have to throw them out because no one wants them. The most important thing is not to keep all these things if you don't have room for them. If you keep them, they'll become a burden instead of a source of pleasant memories on the very rare occasions that you look through them in the future.

Finally, you may make the decision to let things go, but then someone else expresses surprise that you're doing so, and may even insist that you must keep anything that's been passed down in your family. Don't worry about what others think; if they're not willing to keep certain items, they certainly shouldn't expect you to do so. Sometimes this kind of pressure may come from your parents or other older family members. Again, there's no law that you must keep these things. However, if you *do* move them along, you may not want to tell certain people that you've done so. That's your privilege. Discretion is often required to keep peace in a family.

Learning from Experience

Going through someone's estate can be quite a learning experience. When Donald's grandmother passed away, he inherited her long-time home and everything in it. Donald had always been a packrat, so his wife Lila had visions of him loading up trucks full of Grandma's things and bringing them home to their already cluttered house. But she didn't say anything, because he was taking Grandma's death pretty hard.

Donald, a teacher, ended up spending his entire summer vacation going through Grandma's house so it could be sold. He discovered that Grandma kept anything that might be reused someday. He found hundreds of empty mason jars that looked older than he was. She had enough old pie and cake pans to start a commercial bakery. He found two closets full of his late grandfather's clothes (Grandpa died in the 1970s). The sheer quantity of stuff he had to go through and make decisions about that summer resulted in a changed man. He brought home very few items from Grandma's house—just one of Grandpa's Mad-Men-style hats, Grandma's rocking chair and her photo albums— and spent a lot of gas distributing everything else to relatives, the local hospital thrift shop and the dump. The following summer he went through their own house and got rid of things he'd had since childhood. He told Lila, "I love Grandma and I sure miss her, but I don't ever want to do to Tyler what she did to me, leaving all that stuff to go through."

Little Tyler is only two, but Donald is wise to think ahead about what Tyler will have to go through someday if his dad doesn't reform his packrat ways. Who will be burdened with the task of going through *your* things someday if you don't do it yourself? By reducing your belongings (including inherited items), you'll save your own loved ones a lot of trouble eventually.

The Process of Going Through Inherited Belongings

Whenever you're ready to go through your inherited items, you'll proceed just as we did with the other categories in this book. You'll go through everything and put each item into one of four groups:

Pitch old newspapers and magazines, broken items that can't be repaired, clothes that are ripped, faded or moth-eaten, and anything else that's not good enough to donate to charity.

Donate anything useful that you and other family members don't want, including clothes, books, hobby items, and furniture. If your loved one had a favorite cause or charity, send those items wherever that cause or charity will benefit, if possible.

Sell anything of substantial monetary value that you and other family members don't want to keep. Pieces of furniture and home decor can be sold on consignment, so that they take up space in a store instead of your home while you wait for a buyer. If there are a lot of antiques and collectibles, ask an estate sale agent to assess them first. For further information about finding a top-notch estate agent, see my book *How to Clean out Your Parents' House (Without Filling Up Your Own)*.

Keep only a few precious items that remind you of your loved one. Remember to rank groups of items in terms of which ones you like best, and only choose one or two from each group. (Giving up lesser items makes the best items even more special.) Find the items that most remind you of your loved one, and store the very best of them in a special box that you'll keep where you can easily access it on birthdays, anniversaries or just because you feel like it.

If there are other heirs or surviving family members, make sure they each get something to keep that has meaning for them, if at all possible. Try not to leave anyone out.

Ultimately, it's your memories of your loved one that will live in your heart, not their actual belongings. After all, you wouldn't forget your loved one even if you inherited nothing tangible from them. So, after you've set aside those few most important belongings of theirs, let the rest go with a clear conscience and the knowledge that you did your best.

The Challenge of Heirlooms

The distinction between the possessions of late loved ones vs. family heirlooms is time. Long after someone dies, after their belongings are passed to the next generation, their belongings magically turn into heirlooms. Heirlooms are anything passed down in a family that someone believes is too good to give up because an ancestor owned it. This is how people end up with houses full of items they don't use or even really care about that much: because they were inherited, they're sacrosanct. Or so they believe.

All it takes is one person in each generation to make the effort to go through everything someone left behind when they died, set aside a few things for themselves and a few things others in their family want, and then find meaningful places for the rest. But often, no one is willing to do it. Many people think anything passed down in their family is an heirloom, and insist that someone should keep the family heirlooms, but, of course, they rarely nominate themselves for that job.

Unwilling Keeper of the Flame

Angela had always been the most sentimental of the five Williams sisters. So when her dad died, her mother moved into a tiny apartment and gave Grandma's china to Angela, since she had no room for it anymore. When Uncle Louie left his enormous vintage postcard collection to sister Jean, the flight attendant, it ended up in Angela's attic because Jean traveled so much that she didn't have a house to keep it in. Over the years, whenever there was a family heirloom that needed to be kept, it somehow ended up in Angela's house.

One day Angela's husband Dave got great news: he'd been promoted. But his new position required a cross-country move to San Francisco, an expensive city where they'd be getting a smaller house. In between house-hunting trips, Angela and Dave began paring down all their possessions to minimize the amount of belongings that would have to be sent to (and squeezed into) their new home. Using great self-discipline, Angela gave up many things from her childhood and from her children's infancy. Her reward was far fewer boxes for the movers to take....but the large stack of boxes in the attic that held all the family heirlooms she'd been given by family members for safekeeping could not go along for the trip.

Angela called her sisters and her mom, explaining that she couldn't take these things with her and that they would have to pick them up. And suddenly she was awash in excuses: Mom still had no room for the china, Deedee was afraid her boys would break the antique lamps, Jean left a message saying she wouldn't be back in town for weeks and sorry, but what could she do? As for sisters Tina and Tori, they didn't even call back.

As moving day loomed closer, Angela felt her only option was to send out a group text: "If no one comes for the family heirlooms by 3/15, they go to Goodwill. Sorry, I have no choice."

Angela heard nothing from her family until the 14th, when Tina's husband backed up his work truck, loaded up the heirlooms, and took off, after grumbling, "Dunno where we're gonna put these....."

If you're the designated keeper of heirlooms, but you don't use them or really even want them, feel free to move them along. Anyone who tells you that you *must* keep something should keep it at their house instead of using your house for storage. This attitude may not make you popular. But if others are that insistent that the items must be kept, then *they* should keep them.

Usually heirlooms are things that most people really don't use anymore; I guess that's what makes them seem so important historically. But who needs oil lamps when you can flick on a light switch? Who wants the burden of Grandma's hand-painted (can't go in the dishwasher) china, all 20 place settings, when there are dishwasher-safe plates, or even paper plates? What purpose does Uncle Emmett's hand-cranked Victrola serve in a world where you can listen to anything you like on Pandora?

It's sad that these things that were important to our ancestors' daily lives have no use in ours. But that's the way it is; we can't change progress by keeping all this stuff in our attics and basements. It's OK to let them go to someone who wants them, even if that person isn't "in the family."

Ultimately, heirlooms are nice in theory, but most are a burden in reality. Keep a few tiny heirlooms if you really want to; I have some and I treasure them. But as for the big things, the cumbersome things, the china-settings-for-20, don't let anyone guilt you into keeping them. It's hard enough to go through things that *you're* sentimental about without adding to them the things that other people are sentimental about!

Turn Your Heirlooms Into Cash

If you need a second pair of eyes to assess an heirloom, ask someone from the next generation whether they think it should be kept. Miranda did that after she inherited her aunt's substantial jewelry collection. Most of it was costume jewelry, but some items were made of gold or silver; the only thing all the items had in common was that they were large and showy...but then so was Aunt Marge.

Miranda thought she might keep one or two pieces, and pass the rest down to her kids. She asked her son Jared to take a look at the collection the next time he stopped by, thinking maybe he'd like to pick out something for his girlfriend.

Jared did not mince words.

"Mom, you have got to be kidding! That stuff's nasty. No girl wants anything like that."

Miranda was glad Aunt Marge couldn't hear him, but she silently admitted to herself that she didn't see anything she would ever wear in public. Suspecting her other son would have a similar reaction to Jared's, she put the jewelry box back into her closet. But a few weeks later she saw an ad for an auction house that was looking for antique jewelry. In a moment of bravery, she called the number and set up an appointment. In the end, she traded the jewelry for a check that was large enough to divide by three and still make her and her boys very happy.

So, which of *your* heirlooms might be turned into cash?

Preventing Future Guilt

Older relatives (especially your parents) will often protest if you suggest that they get rid of any family heirloom, because they may have memories of the item, the person who owned it or both. This is to be expected, but it doesn't change the fact that once they pass the items on to you, you won't be obligated to keep them unless you have the desire and the space to do so.

People often keep far too much stuff because they won't or can't go through it all. But years later, after they've passed away, their heirs assume that *all* their belongings meant something to them, so they feel guilty getting rid of any of them. If you can find out for certain which items your parents or other older relatives love the most or feel the most sentimental about, you'll be able to go through their estate someday with much less guilt, getting rid of all sorts of things you know for certain weren't important to them, and saving your decision-making energy for the items they loved most. So take the opportunity soon to ask them which of their belongings are most important to them.

Some people aren't comfortable talking about this. But you'll save a lot of wear and tear on your future emotions if you can get older family members to discuss such things now. And you may learn, as Brad did, that older people often keep far too much stuff for reasons other than sentimentality.

When Brad's mom finally admitted that she could no longer care for her large old farmhouse because of age-related physical problems, he convinced her that it was time to move to a smaller place. He took a week off of work and flew in alone so that he could help her go through the house and determine which items would be coming with her to her new home. He had great plans for tackling all three stories' worth of stuff methodically, but he didn't count on his mother standing over him pleading, "No, not those! Please, I might need them!" Items of special significance to her included dusty, cracked shoes from the 1970s, a large collection of gravy boats, and at least three dozen vases and planters that once held flowers or plants sent to her for birthdays, Mother's Day and Christmas. It became clear to Brad that he would have to do this job alone if it was going to get done at all.

So he spent a day moving his mother into her new apartment with just the basics: clothes, furniture and her televisions. Then he went back to the house and spent the rest of the week alone, going through as much as he could before it was time to fly home. On the way to the airport, he stopped by the apartment to say good-bye. He braced himself for all sorts of questions about what had been going on at the house, but before he could say anything, his mother gave him a big hug.

"Thank you so much for moving me in here. I think it's just the cutest place, and I love how you arranged everything!" She beamed.

"Well, Mom, next time I come in, I'll try to finish going through the house and the rest of your things. There's just so much of it...." he began.

"No hurry, son. I don't even miss most of it. To tell the truth, I'm rather relieved. I spent years worrying about what to do with all of it, and now you've made the decisions for me. I feel free as a bird!"

Brad's jaw dropped. He spent the flight home calculating what size rental truck he should back up to the farmhouse when he returned in a month or so, and whether it would fit under the covered Goodwill donation drive-up.

What Would Grandma Do?

For sentimental people, giving up items that were inherited from family members isn't just about letting go of the belongings, but letting go of the people we loved and lost. In time, this gets easier, especially if we find ways to give their things to people who either need or will appreciate them.

Surely our family members never wanted to overwhelm us with tons of their belongings. In truth, *they* may have been overwhelmed by *their own* belongings, or they never got the time to go through it all, or they became ill before they could do so. One clue as to which items they actually cared about is whether or not something was packed carefully. If you find a crocheted bedspread packed lovingly in a fancy box lined with clean tissue paper, you can assume that Grandma treasured that bedspread and would want it to go somewhere special. As for the hundreds of dusty old boxes full of random stuff that you found in her attic, basement and garage, she probably just never got around to them and wouldn't care where you sent them. Maybe she was as overwhelmed with her accumulated stuff as you are, and would have pitched every last dusty box if she'd had the energy.

As for which inherited items you should keep for yourself, something that you'll use regularly or that brings back great memories for you is your best bet. Don't save things in case your children should want them someday; they may not want anything that was passed down through the family. If your children are old enough, ask them if there's anything in the estate that interests them.

Remember, whatever doesn't interest you or your offspring can be given to interested relatives. (Dispersing such things at family reunions often works well.) Otherwise, finding someone else who truly wants each item by selling it or donating it to a good cause will ease any pain and guilt you may have over letting the items leave your family.

Gifts and Other Expensive Items

A gift can be valuable (a diamond ring) or it can be extremely valuable (the first drawing your child ever made for you). Only you can determine the true value of the gifts you've been given.

In an affluent society like ours, if we kept every gift anyone ever gave us, we'd need a warehouse. Fortunately, many gifts are eventually forgotten, so we don't keep the majority of them. But sentimental people tend to keep too many gifts, not just because they were gifts but because they're reminders of the givers.

If you're a person who puts a lot of effort into picking out gifts, you may assume others do the same, but that's not necessarily so. Some givers are generous people who buy something nice or expensive to show that they care for you, then proceed to mark you off that year's gift list. They may not even remember what they gave you. You might be offended if someone else got rid of a gift you gave them; that doesn't mean others will be devastated if you get rid of something they gave you.

People usually give us gifts in hopes that they'll be used and appreciated. So if you're not using or appreciating items that you've kept for years just because they're gifts, why not pass them along to someone who will actually use them? There's no law that says you have to keep something just because it was a gift.

Remember, the gift-giver simply wanted to do something nice for you. Most likely, they didn't intend that you should keep the gift forever. (If they did, it wasn't a gift but an obligation.) Had they known their gift would become a burden, they surely would tell you to pass it on.

Ultimately, you'll have to judge each gift on the basis of whether you love it, whether you need it and whether you have room for it. Since you're decluttering, you must not have enough open space and storage space in your house, so you're making room by getting rid of things you no longer find useful and beautiful (remember William Morris?) That's why your goal is to keep only your most treasured gifts, and to pass the rest along to others who will treasure them, too.

Wedding Gifts

One type of gift that can be particularly hard to give up is wedding gifts. Young couples may not understand this, because today most wedding gifts come in the form of cash, checks or items they themselves chose for their registry. But many people who were married in the 20th century have wedding gifts chosen by the givers that they've never used, taking up space in cabinets, closets, basements and attics.

An acquaintance of mine we'll call Velma has an attic full of wedding gifts she hasn't looked at in many years, and she was married in the late 1950s! She recalls a glass cocktail set and a tea set, but says there are many other gifts up there; it's so hard to get into her attic that she hasn't seen these items in years. Let's be logical: if you haven't used a wedding gift by your 50th anniversary, feel free to give it up! Even monogrammed glassware can be useful to someone else.

You don't have to keep wedding gifts for a certain amount of time after the wedding, either. Catelyn got married in her mid-20s; her elderly grandparents' wedding gift to her and her new husband Sean was one of their four sets of china. Sixteen place settings trimmed in platinum (hand-wash only) totaled nearly 100 pieces of very breakable dishware for a young couple with a tiny apartment and busy careers. Her grandparents meant well, but to Catelyn and Sean, those dishes were a huge burden. They parked the boxes in the spare bedroom for a few years, wondering what to do with it all. Then they learned that they were going to have a baby. The spare room would now become the baby's room.

Eager to get the china out so she could decorate and bring in a crib, Catelyn took some of the china to a consignment store, where there were rows and rows of china place settings. But the owner wasn't interested; she already had far more china than she could sell. Modern young couples had no use for china, she lamented.

So Catelyn tried **craigslist.org** in the fall, before the holidays, hoping someone was looking for new dishes to use while hosting holiday meals. No one responded, so she brought the price down weekly; still there were no takers.

Her mother suggested a website where you could sell unwanted china, but the details on the website made it clear that you'd have to spend a small fortune packing everything up so it would (hopefully) arrive unbroken. Catelyn and Sean couldn't afford that, especially with a baby on the way.

So Sean loaded all the china into Catelyn's car, and she drove to a religious charity's thrift store (which had a drive-up donation area), where she donated all of the china, feeling afterward as though the weight of the world had been lifted from her shoulders. She had warned her mother ahead of time that she planned to do this, and her mother understood, saying only, "Don't tell anyone in the family, anyone. And do *not* put it on Facebook!" So far, Catelyn has kept quiet. She just hopes Grandma never asks her about the china.

Gift Guilt

Even gifts you've accumulated over the years that you didn't use or didn't care about may be impossible for you to give up, just because they were gifts, and you feel guilty about getting rid of gifts. Try looking at each gift in light of these questions:

- Do you even remember who gave it to you, or just that it was a gift?

- Do you use it? If not, why not? Will you start using it if the alternative is giving it up?

- Can you give it to someone who would love it, such as a child, grandchild or dear friend?

- Can you take a photo of it and then donate it to your favorite charity?

Remember, a gift *represents* the affection the giver had and/or has for you; it does not equate it. And if the giver is no longer in your life, you won't disrespect their memory by giving away any of their gifts to you.

If this is a struggle for you because you want to keep *all* the gifts just because they were gifts, even though you don't use them, grouping the gifts and ranking them in order of their importance to you (as we've done with other categories) probably won't work. Even if you keep the top one or two items, you won't want to give up the rest because of gift guilt. You'll probably have to spend a little more time thinking about what to do.

While you're at it, reread the list of questions above, and then consider this advice from Leo Babauta (**zenhabits.net**):

> Free yourself of this guilt. Your loved ones gave you the gifts to make you happy, not to burden you for life, not to make you feel guilty. Allow yourself to be happy, and only keep things if they're making you happy.

Consider also that by sharing those items with others, you're honoring the memory of the love that was behind the gift.

Finally, if you don't even remember who gave you a gift, feel free to get rid of it. Conversely, if the mere sight of a gift brings sweet memories of the giver flooding back to you, consider keeping that item, especially if it's small, and putting it where you will see it every day.

Handmade Gifts

The gift guilt load seems to double when it comes to handmade gifts. That's understandable. The giver must have cared a lot for you to put their time into making something for you, so the gift was a token of their esteem. If the gift is something you still use and can't bear to part with, keep it. If someone put a lot of work into something and you liked it and kept it around for quite a while, but you no longer use it or have room for it, consider passing it along to someone who can use it, or if it's worth cash, give it to a charity you like that can turn it into cash.

When my late aunt reached middle age, she took up ceramics as a hobby. For years after that, we were all given painted figurines each Christmas. I only kept those figurines for a few years; I don't even remember what we did with them. But I still remember that she made them for us, so I have the memories even if I don't have the items. However, she also made a large ceramic Christmas tree with tiny plastic light bulbs and gave it to us for a wedding gift. Nearly 40 years later, we still have that tree. It's cumbersome to store, but we put it out every Christmas and it has become part of my own family's Christmas memories. Whenever I see it, I think of my aunt.

We hate to give up a handmade gift because we're sure the creator would be disappointed to know that we did so. As a creator, I can assure you that's true. You may have guessed (from my multiple references to turning clothes into quilts) that I am a quilter. I've made many quilts for family members, and I hate the thought that they might ever get rid of them. That said, the quilts belong to them now and they can do what they wish with them (I don't want to know!) Of course, fabric fades and wears out over time, so it's understandable that at some point, their quilts won't be useful anymore. (Hmmm, then they'll need new ones. I've got just the pattern!) Anyways, I know how it feels to make something special for someone, but I certainly wouldn't want to burden them with what I intend to be a gift, so I wouldn't want them to keep my quilts just out of obligation. I like to think that if someone gets rid of a quilt I made, they'll give it or sell it to someone who loves how it looks.

Expensive Gifts

Sometimes we receive gifts that are quite expensive, so we keep them even if they're not our taste, or if they're in our way, just because they cost a lot. Again, the giver esteemed you enough to spend a lot of money on you, but that still doesn't mean you must keep the item forever. The item itself, or at least its market value, thrilled you at one time. The giver's goal was to make you happy, so it worked.

But if you don't need the item anymore, or never really used it and don't intend to, pass it on or sell it while accepting that the giver's goal was met; he or she made you happy when they gave the gift to you.

If you no longer need or use an expensive gift, consider re-gifting it. Years ago, I dated a young man who gave me a lovely gift. Knowing I especially liked the work of artist Norman Rockwell, he gave me a large, beautifully matted and framed Rockwell print of a couple getting engaged. I was delighted with it. (Though if it was a hint, it didn't work, as we broke up the following year.) When I married my husband a few years later, he didn't want the print (which I still liked) in our first home together. Meanwhile, my mother had gotten used to having the print in the house from when I lived at home. The scene reminded her of when she and my father became engaged years ago; she said that day she even wore a dress similar to the one the girl in the print wore. So I gave the print to my mother, and it has been hers for many more years than it was ever mine. She's elderly now, and downsized into a condo years ago, but that print made the cut and now hangs in my parents' bedroom. I'm glad she's enjoyed it all these years, and I enjoy seeing it again when I visit them.

Often, an expensive gift that you no longer need can be donated to a charity you financially support, so that it now becomes a very generous gift to a cause you care about. That will make both the charity and you happy. Thus the original giver's gift made you happy twice: once when it was given to you, and again when you used it to help your favorite charity. Win, win!

Occasionally, expensive gifts come with strings. Your sister has been bugging you for weeks to take her three untrained Pomeranians into your home while she goes on vacation because she doesn't trust kennels. You've been balking. Suddenly she gifts you with a large and expensive lamp you don't need or have room for. Hmmm....sounds suspicious. Keep the doggie decision separate from the guilt trip she's trying to take you on, and feel free to re-gift or sell the bait.

Some gift givers may be generous, but their gift-giving masks their control issues. Joanie's mother-in-law frequently gave her and her family new appliances they didn't really need, new pieces of furniture that weren't their style, and large plastic climbing toys for the kids that clogged up their family room. With her eagle eyes, "Meemaw" always noticed if one of her gifts was missing, even if it had just been moved down to the basement. Joanie often told friends that if she got rid of something her mother-in-law had given them, she was sure Meemaw's internal radar would send off sirens in her head at that very moment, wherever she might be.

If you suspect this is why you've been given expensive gifts you neither needed nor wanted, feel free to give them away or sell them. Why should you have to trip over the giver's expensive controlling devices? Then brace yourself for impact. The giver has issues that are not your fault. If you get rid of enough of their expensive but unwanted gifts, maybe they'll give up on this tactic.

Expensive Belongings

What about expensive items that you bought for yourself but no longer love or use? You think to yourself, "I paid a lot for this. I can't just let it go for pennies!" And back it goes into one of your storage areas, eating up space that you would prefer to free up for other, more beloved items, or even to keep as open, uncluttered areas.

We work hard for our money, and we hate to let go of things that cost us a lot. Often those purchases are good memories, too, so our sentimental nature pushes us toward keeping them.

Years ago, when it was just the two of us, my husband and I used to walk around a very large mall near our home. We'd hold hands and stroll through different stores, not usually buying anything but just enjoying the rare free time together when neither of us had to be at work. One of our favorite stops was an art gallery where prints of all sorts were sold.

It was only natural that certain artists and their works would become our favorites. Once we bought our first house, we'd often go into this gallery and discuss which pieces of art we would like to put in our house someday when we had the money. There were some I loved, and some my husband loved. After a few years of home ownership, we splurged on a couple of large, expensive prints. They graced the walls of our homes for many years.

Then we downsized to the little house we live in now. Not only do we not have enough wall space for those large prints, but their scale, which fit the rooms in our previous houses, is too overwhelming for the small rooms in this house. So we put the prints in our storage area, thinking at some point we might move to a larger home again and would have the right places to hang those prints.

That was six years ago. It doesn't appear that we'll be moving anytime soon, and even if we do, we've found that we love the freedom of a small house (much less time spent cleaning, much less money spent maintaining) and will probably *not* move to a larger house if we ever move again. So I'm thinking it's time to sell those prints if none of our children want them. Yes, we did spend a lot of money on them, and I doubt that we'll get much of it back if we sell them. But they aren't doing anyone any good stacked against a wall in the basement, and I'll always have the memory of when we bought them. Time to move them on.

If your decluttering efforts include your entire house, don't try to decide what to do with your expensive but unneeded items right now. Set them aside to deal with later. Determining what to do with each one can really slow you down. Besides, seeing them all in one group later on may make it easier for you to give up most or all of them.

Displaying the Best Gifts and Expensive Items

When choosing which gifts and expensive items you will keep, consider where you'll use or display them. If you have items (like our art prints) that are too large in size or scale for your home, it might be best to move them along while keeping other, smaller items. The reverse is also true. If you have a large open wall or display cabinet, keep a few larger, more striking pieces for those areas and reduce your supply of smaller items.

Keeping too many expensive items that you bought can backfire on you; if you aren't still crazy about them, they're just a visual reminder of how much you spent (maybe overspent?) and how you wish you had that money back. Try to accept that the person you were at the time got great pleasure out of buying those things. You enjoyed them for a long while, but now you don't, so give them up and let someone else enjoy them. If you get some money for them, great. But if not, the pleasure you got from them back in the day is worth something, right? Such items can always go to consignment stores, where they'll be on display, most likely for a while. So if you change your mind, you know where to find your items and can always get them back. Most likely, you won't do that, though, because your taste has changed.

You can also donate such belongings to a charity or a church that auctions off expensive items for fundraisers. You'll be helping out a group you care about, and you may even be able to take the donation as a tax deduction.

Once you reduce your load down to the very most precious gifts and expensive items, consider rotating them if you have more than you can use or display at one time. Put some in storage; after the others have been on display for a while, swap them out. This keeps your home from looking cluttered, and it's a nice change to look at something different every so often. This will only work if you have the storage space, of course. Otherwise, you have kept too much!

Learning from Letting Go of Gifts and Expensive Items

After you've given up expensive items that were given to you, you realize that while it's great to be generous to others, it might be wiser to gift people with experiences rather than things. That way they can enjoy what you've given them, but they won't ever be burdened by an item that you might love more than they do. Another option is to give cash; it doesn't take up much space but it's always appreciated! If you must give a tangible gift, and you want to be extra generous, try to make the expensive gift a practical one. Pay for the crib your new grandchild needs, or buy your grandpa the lift chair he's been talking about. Expensive impractical gifts become burdens rather quickly, sometimes instantly.

As for expensive items you bought for yourself, you might consider just giving them away to others. They'll either love the item, or the money they can get for it if they sell it. Since you're unlikely to get back what you paid for it if you were to sell it, no lesser amount would make you feel good about the situation. But if giving it away makes someone else happy, the knowledge that it did so may be worth more to you than money. Think about it.

Collections

Everyday Collections

As we go about our daily lives, we naturally begin to amass certain belongings, and they become a collection whether we realize it or not. Our clothes become a collection, our kitchenware becomes a collection, our photos (from back when we all printed out photos) became a collection, etc. The problem with sentimental people is that we often become attached to our everyday collections. Not all of them, mind you. For instance, even though I love to garden, I have no great emotional attachment to my collection of gardening tools and supplies, many of which I've used for decades. Yet I keep far too many linens, towels and bedding around, and occasionally have to force myself to weed through it all and get rid of the faded, torn or otherwise bedraggled items because I'm attached to them.

When we downsized, I had a very hard time giving up our sizable collection of twin-sized sheet sets. None of my kids wanted them; they had moved out and had queen- or king-sized beds, so they had no interest in twin-sized sheets. But I associated good memories of my children with those sheets, blankets and bedspreads, so it took a while for me to reduce my linens collection to just what we use in our downsized home. I also kept a few especially cute twin sheet sets that I saved for future grandchildren. (My little grandson, two states away, now sleeps on those sheets.)

Clearly, sentimental people often have a harder time going through some everyday collections than others because their nature makes them want to keep *anything* with a memory attached to it.

As discussed in a previous chapter, many people collect books (we like to call them personal libraries), which can easily become a large, cumbersome collection. Here are some other everyday collections we might be attached to, along with tips for reducing them:

Christmas Decorations and Old Christmas Cards

This group is a land mine for sentimental people. Most Christmas decorations have lovely memories attached to them. After all, Christmas is usually a time of family gatherings, great food (including favorite family recipes) and gift exchanges. Even people who aren't all that sentimental will hang onto old tree ornaments or wall decorations because they remind them of past Christmases. There's nothing wrong with that. But over the years, we tend to accumulate more Christmas decorations than we can display, so if it's been years since you weeded through your Christmas decorations, now is the time to reduce your collection.

You may find that the items you use every year are at the top of the storage containers or boxes, and the items that have languished untouched for years are at the bottom. Remove the decorations you haven't used in years, as well as broken ornaments that can't be fixed, or that you don't care enough about to fix. Tatty garlands should go straight to the trash. Decorations that still have life in them might be appreciated by local nursing homes, or you can donate them to the Goodwill, Salvation Army or another thrift shop of your choice.

Once you've eliminated the items you haven't used in years, and the broken items, consolidate what's left so that you don't need so many storage containers. Doing so will free up space in your storage area.

Some people do Christmas up very big, with multiple Christmas trees, multiple rooms of decorations and enough ornaments to start their own Christmas shop. If that describes you, and you enjoy doing so much decorating each year (not to mention the process of carefully packing up everything after the festivities), so be it. But if it has become a burden to you, why not reduce your load down to one tree's worth, one room's worth, and donate the rest? You can always take those boxes full of holiday cheer to a community center in a disadvantaged part of town where others can enjoy them.

Another good time to winnow down your Christmas collection is right after the holiday. You'll know which items were used and which items sat in a storage box through the Christmas season. You'll be aware of which light sets are shot, and which still work. Excess ornaments, tree skirts, and star or angel tree toppers will still be in storage, too. Clear out the unused items; everything you take down after Christmas can then go into the empty storage boxes. Remember, Christmas decorations that sit in storage during the holidays aren't bringing Christmas cheer to anyone.

As for Christmas cards, they're slowly disappearing from the scene as more people use the Internet to send holiday greetings. Nevertheless, there are still some diehards out there (I'm one of them) who send Christmas cards to family and friends every year, often with a family photo tucked in. Many of us have collected those cards and photos over the years, and are reluctant to get rid of them; even those braggy Christmas letters people used to send include aspects of our family history that we hate to throw away.

If you kept Christmas cards from previous years, go through and separate out the cards from people you're no longer close to and throw them in your recycle bin or the garbage. Then go through the rest, keeping only those cards, photos and letters that really mean something to you. Put them in a fancy Christmas box for safe-keeping; if space is at a premium, scan them and keep them on your computer instead. Some sentimental people punch holes in the corners of their special Christmas cards and photos and hang them (and only them) on a table-sized Christmas tree each year. What a lovely way to enjoy and share Christmas memories!

Greeting Cards, Birthday Cards, and Letters

Like Christmas cards, greeting and birthday cards are also in decline. As for letters, they were overtaken by email years ago. That said, there are still people who write letters or make and send cards, and if you cherish those items and will go through them again, they're worth scanning or even keeping in a special box. But most cards these days arrive with just a signature on them, and don't need to be kept. The fact that someone took the time to send you a greeting is the good part; the card itself is extraneous. So throw it out without guilt, while keeping gratitude for the sender in your heart.

As for letters, if you have a collection of letters that are very special to you, and you actually reread them from time to time, scan them to preserve them even if you keep the actual letters. That way, if they're accidentally destroyed, you can still reread them.

Some letter collections are not meant to be kept. While going through our many, many boxes of belongings when we downsized, my husband and I found a box of love letters we exchanged while on different college campuses at the beginning of our relationship. We had duct-taped the box shut years ago to keep our kids out of it. Now we were faced with the decision of whether to keep it or not. After reading a few of the letters, we agreed that their personal nature dictated that we shred them rather than risk our adult kids reading them some day when going through our estate.

Other couples who don't want to leave their love letters behind have burned them, or have shredded them and thrown them in a hole in their yard just before planting a tree in it. So consider the nature of your precious letter collection(s) and whether you care if anyone else eventually reads them, before you decide to keep them.

Photo Collections

Most of us have photo collections. While in recent years, we've probably taken and kept our photos on digital cameras, phones and computers, we still have many photos from the years before we began fully relying on digital photography. These photos are slowly deteriorating. In fact, the oldest photos, from 50 years ago or more, may have held up better than photos from the late 20th century.

It takes time, and will be an ongoing process, but your best bet is to go through your photos, keep the best and pitch the rest, and then scan the keepers. You can store them online in places like **Flickr.com** or **Dropbox.com**. (You'll want to use more than one site in case one of them suddenly goes out of business.) When storing photos on the cloud, usually there's a limit for free storage, so if you have a lot of photos, you might have to pay monthly.

You can also store photos on your computer, a memory card, CD, DVD or a flash drive. Ideally, store them on the cloud *and* on a physical device: if you lose your password, you may lose access to your photos, so a physical back-up would be a lifesaver in that situation.

Using services like **Shutterfly.com** lets you make gifts with your scanned or digital photos for family and friends. We have a calendar filled with photos of our grandchildren that our daughter-in-law made for us using Shutterfly. What a great gift idea: it displays those we love in a form that doesn't take up much space in our little house.

If you're not into technology, keep photos in acid-free boxes and/or albums to help preserve them. If you find family photos that don't mean much to you but might interest a relative, be sure to give them to them. Keep your photo collection where you can easily access it, not just in case of fire or flood, but so that you get in the habit of regularly going through your photos. Otherwise, what's the point of keeping them?

Art Collections

Some people have virtually nothing on their walls, but sentimental people often display a wide variety of art and decorations in their homes. Sometimes these pieces are the result of our travels, which come with good memories, or are from our childhood homes or from relatives who have passed on, making them sentimental favorites even if we no longer have room for them.

If you have far too many pieces of artwork to fit comfortably in your home, separate the "must keep" items from the "wish I could keep" items. Then take digital photos of the latter group before giving them away or selling them. As I mentioned earlier (regarding the Rockwell print I re-gifted to my mother), if you give a piece of artwork to a family member or friend who loves it, you can see it whenever you visit them.

To make it easier to determine which pieces are your very favorites, put some away for a while and see if you even miss them. Absence might make the heart grow fonder, or it might make you forget.

If you have framed paintings or photographs that are just starting to fade, or that you don't have room to display, you can take them to Staples or another store with a copying service and have them scanned. You can then use them as wallpaper on a computer monitor, or just keep the scans with your (hopefully growing) collection of digital photographs of things you love but moved along while decluttering.

After Greg's divorce, he was left with all the artwork but no house. His new place was much smaller, and there wasn't enough room to display all of the artwork. So he chose the most appropriate pieces for each room and hung them up. Then he took digital photos of the rest, used a paint program on his computer to reduce them to less than a foot square each, printed them and framed them. They now hang in a large grouping on his foyer wall, where he can see and enjoy them every day. He sold the original pieces on **ArtBrokerage.com.**

Music Collections

Music collections are especially sentimental because they remind us of important times of our lives. Music is so evocative; it can take you back as though a day hadn't passed, much less years. But the methods for transmitting music have changed: from record albums, to eight-track tapes, to cassette tapes, to CD's, to MP3's...and now some people are buying record albums again.

But for most of us, older forms of recorded music are cumbersome and take up too much valuable space. Recently I attended an estate sale in an old mansion. The late owner's huge den was ringed with shelves full of record albums. They were mostly 1950's and 1960's jazz albums. They were priced at $10 each; while there were lookers, I didn't see anyone buying any. Most of us no longer have stereo systems on which to play record albums.

Fortunately music is now available on the Internet, often for free. So if you're emotionally attached to your 45 rpm recording of the Monkees' "I'm a Believer," sign up at **Pandora.com** and create a Monkees station (take a photo of the 45 if you must before giving it up). **YouTube.com** is another free source of music from around the world.

If you have a large music collection but no longer have the means to listen to it, it's time to reduce your collection and replace it with forms that you can enjoy. If you have a CD player, replace your old tapes or records with CDs. If you prefer to listen online, buy the music files online, too. The latest methods of musical recording let you have a huge collection of music without taking up any space in your home, and bluetooth speakers are often unobtrusive but play as well as those giant speakers you once had.

Readers with tech skills can transfer their music collections to digital form and save some money in the process. This article describes how to do so:

https://www.cnet.com/how-to/the-cheap-way-to-convert-lps-audio-cassettes-to-digital

Of course, you may not want to replace everything in your music collection; we often outgrow or tire of certain artists or genres. There's nothing wrong with that; just admit it to yourself and pull such items out of your collection. Donate your old records (unless they're warped), tapes (unless they're tangled or heat-damaged), and CDs (unless they're scratched), or sell them online, at a garage sale or on **craigslist.org** (be sure to include the names of the artists to attract those who are searching for them).

Wardrobes

Sentimental people tend to keep their old clothes even as they add new clothes to their closets. The result is a collection of clothes that stretches back for years. Many pieces bring back memories of who we were, or of who we had hoped to become.

But clothes rarely get better with age. Over time most fabrics fade, rot, and attract insects. Certain items may remind you of happy times in the past, but you cannot recapture those days by wearing the items (*if* they still fit). Take a photo of the item if you don't already have a photo of you wearing it years ago, and then move it on.

As noted earlier, you can always make (or have someone else make) a pillow or quilt out of old clothes that have great meaning to you. **Etsy.com** is a good place to find someone to do that for you.

That said, some classic clothes are worth keeping if they're made exceptionally well and of high-quality fabric. If they still fit you (or can be altered to fit), and you really will wear them, keep them.

Reducing your wardrobe down to the very best items will leave you with room in your closet and around your clothes, which keeps them fresh. Fewer clothes means fewer decisions each morning. Keep clothes that go well together so that you can create a variety of looks from a limited number of pieces.

Reread Deanna's story in chapter 5 if you need encouragement in this area.

Linens and Bedding

Most houses have linen closets, which makes this category seem like a collection. But modern bedding is usually pretty large, because more people have queen- or king-sized beds. Modern mattresses are also quite tall, so bedding takes up even more room than it once did. As a result, many of us have more linens and bedding than we can fit in a linen closet.

I love linens and bedding, and thanks to our large family, I had a very large collection that I had to cull when we downsized. This was a challenge, because I believe that older towels last longer, and that the fabric in older sheets, blankets and bedspreads is often of better quality (and prettier) than what is sold in most stores today.

I separated the items by category, and then went through them, keeping only the very best items that we still used regularly. This greatly reduced our collection. Since our hall linen closet is tiny, I only put towels in it. I then put the bedding on the closet shelves of the room in which it's used. (I keep bedding in large plastic boxes with lavender sachets for freshness; I don't put lids on the boxes, so that air can get to the bedding.)

When you store bedding in the bedrooms, you're left with plenty of room in the linen closet.

Videotapes and DVDs

It's hard to find a VCR for sale these days, but many of us still have our old VCRs and plenty of tapes, both store-bought and home-recorded. We may even watch them once in a while. But videotapes take up a lot of space and lose picture quality over time. Weed out those tapes you no longer watch or care about and donate them (if you can find a place that will still take them), give them away or throw them out. As for the rest, replace those you love with DVDs if possible. (We are old movie lovers and kept dozens of old movies that are not available on DVD.) Of course you can also buy many movies online now that can be instantly downloaded and kept in your device or computer.

Videos and DVDs were one area I really struggled with when I first began the decluttering process. We had literally hundreds of them. Many were my children's favorites that they no longer wanted but that I was emotionally attached to because of the memories. Some were special programs I had recorded for myself over the years. Once I tried to watch a few of them, I had to acknowledge they were deteriorating. This experience helped me get rid of most of them. I did keep a few special favorites that aren't available on DVD and were in good shape (we have a DVD/video player so I can still watch them), and I replaced several others with DVD versions.

Our collection of family video recordings presented a special problem: once I finally realized that videotapes deteriorate, I panicked because I didn't know how to save our precious videos of our family as it grew. One of my adult children came to the rescue, telling me to send our tapes to Yes Video (**yesvideo.com**). They put our movies on an online account, where we could see them and edit them. Then they turned our edited movies into DVDs, which I now treasure. As a bonus, they take up far less space than the videotapes did, and will last much longer. Yes Video also offers options for watching your movies online, on your phone or on other devices. I highly recommend them!

If you're able to weed out a substantial number of DVDs (movies you're tired of, duplicates, television series you won't watch again) from your collection, and they're still in good shape, you can sell them online. However, you may not get as much money as you'd like for the effort, which will include packing and shipping. Many people sell their DVDs on **Amazon.com** or **eBay.com**, and find that they can make good money on popular items, but that the majority of DVDs only bring in a few dollars. You can also trade DVDs for Amazon gift cards at **Amazon.com**. Go here for more details: **https://www.amazon.com/Amazon-Trade-In/b?ie=UTF8&node=9187220011**

Hobby Supply Collections

If you're an artist or hobbyist, you know just how easily art and craft supplies multiply. Many of us believe that having a wealth of materials on hand actually spurs on creativity, so we buy paints, scrapbook paper or fabric whenever we need a bit of inspiration. But over time, these items accumulate and take up a lot of space. If we're honest with ourselves, not all of it is even that inspiring to us anymore. When things reach that point, it's time to go through it all and weed out what no longer inspires, even though our first thought is, "But I might need this later!" or "It's still usable!" Keep in mind that others might find it inspiring even if you no longer do; one of the busiest areas of my local Goodwill store is the craft aisle.

Once you weed out the stuff you aren't inspired by or aren't likely to use anytime soon, you'll make room for future objects of inspiration that you're sure to find along the way. In the meantime, there's nothing like a nice, clean, uncluttered work area to make you want to get started on a fresh, new project.

(If you have plenty of supplies but haven't practiced your hobby in many years, or maybe never did but always intended to, see the next chapter for additional help.)

Toy Collections

When you discover that your young child enjoys a certain type of toy, it's only natural to get them more of it because we like to make our kids happy. So once we see little Brayden contentedly playing with a small toy car, we pick up small cars whenever we're out shopping, we tell Grandma to add to his car collection when she asks for birthday ideas, and we start looking for storage and display options for small cars on **Pinterest.com**.

Then someday when Brayden is too old and too busy playing video games to care about his small car collection, which now takes up several carrying cases and a wall display unit, we will struggle with the idea of getting rid of the collection because we remember him pushing that first tiny car around the kitchen floor while going, "Vroom! Vroom!"

This principle also holds true for dolls, action figures, Legos, and any other toys that tend to be similar in nature or are issued in updated or new versions.

Generally, we adults tend to feel more sentimental about keeping such collections than our kids do. So don't even begin to go through a toy collection until you find out if your child (young or adult) even wants to keep the collection. If they don't, you shouldn't, either. Move it along! But if the child still wants it, keep it a while longer if your child is young, but send it with him or her if your child is an adult. What they do with it is their business. Besides, you probably have enough of your own collections to deal with.

Sentimental Collections

In addition to becoming attached to some of their everyday collections, sentimental people are particularly susceptible to establishing and growing collections for the fun of it.

We may begin collecting something because it strikes a chord within us. Often that chord is a sentimental feeling toward a time or place that the collection represents. Perhaps you began collecting little ceramic cows because your grandma had a cow on her farm and you cherish that memory. Or maybe you loved music as a young teen, and your modest collection of 45's morphed into an album collection that grew throughout your teens, and then you lugged it to college, where it expanded further. By the time you were a young adult with your first home, your album collection filled an entire wall of shelves and had become the physical representation of the soundtrack of your life.

Sometimes the subject of the collection simply appeals to you; perhaps you fell in love with Precious Moments figurines the first time you ever saw them, and had to have one. Then the collecting began; new ones came out that were even cuter than the first one, and you started hinting to friends and family for more as your birthday approached. You just couldn't resist those pale pastel figures with the over-sized heads. Something about them captivated you.

Or maybe someone started you on a collection when you were young and it feels like something you need to keep, even though you've outgrown it. For example, David's dad used to bring him beer bottle caps from his worldwide business travels; David's collection of bottle caps is now so huge that he feels it would be a shame to give it up, even though he personally hates the taste of beer.

There is almost nothing humans won't collect. Did you know people collect salt and pepper shakers? Hotel room key cards? Umbrella cover sleeves? Banana stickers? Airsick bags? (Unused, of course!)

What is it that attracts us to collecting groups of like items? I think our interest in the item is part of it, but the thrill of the hunt is what keeps it going. It's exciting to find something to add to our collection. Even though it may not actually be useful (what can you do with banana stickers, seriously?), each item acquired grows the collection, so it has a purpose, at least in our eyes.

Others approve because it makes it easy for them to find things to give us. ("I know Eunice's birthday is tomorrow and I didn't buy a gift yet, but I'll just pick up a potholder to add to her collection and she'll be over the moon!") If our collection isn't too cumbersome, even our spouse and family won't mind having it around. In fact, they probably have their own growing collections.

There are companies whose sole purpose is to tempt people who are collectors. You see their so-called collectibles in women's magazines and on television shopping networks. These companies create dolls, figurines, decorative plates, sports-team related memorabilia and the like, and their advertising claims that such items are collectible and unique (not to mention easily purchased via several "easy monthly payments"). While insisting that the items are only available for a limited time, such companies regularly come out with more similar items. Their advertising makes you feel like you have to have the latest model in order to "complete" the collection....until the next one comes out. Amassing one of these collections will cost you a fair amount of money on shipping and handling in addition to the cost of each item itself.

However we acquired a collection, they're fun, and they give us something to talk about, think about and make plans for the future. ("I can't wait until they come out with the latest Beanie Baby!" said almost every little girl at some point during the 1990s.) But over time, we often begin to tire of a collection. It no longer makes us as happy as it once did. The law of diminishing returns has kicked in: each successive addition turns us on a little less than the one before. We adored the first one we bought, we found more and they were awesome, too...but after a while, as we add more and more, they all start to look the same, even though they each differ in some small way. And if the collection is large, we eventually tire of dusting it, moving it around or even looking at it. So we pack it up and put it away, rarely thinking about it until we need the space it's taking up. But even then, because we put all that time, effort and money into acquiring the collection, we don't feel that we can give it up. If we're really brave, we decide that we'll only give it up if we can keep it together.

Giving Up a Collection

Getting rid of an entire collection isn't easy, especially if you want to keep it together *and* you want to be paid for it. That's not a problem for most sentimental people, though; the collection represents a happy time in our past, so we don't usually look at it in terms of dollars and cents.

If we inherited a collection, we might feel that we must keep it because it was a gift, or because it was a family heirloom. That was the case with Marie. She inherited her father's collection of decorative glass oil lamps: 57 of them, to be exact. They're all quite similar, made of pastel colored glass and very breakable. They collect dust like mad, so years ago, Marie hired a handyman to create a huge floor-to-ceiling display case in her family room. It has six long, sturdy shelves, and sliding glass doors to keep out the dust. Sometimes Marie imagines having the use of that wall so that she can rearrange the furniture. But what would she do with Daddy's collection? So there they sit, all 57 glass oil lamps, looming over the family room.

Perhaps you inherited a collection and added to it; now you have time and expense invested in it as well as the memories of your loved one. However your collection started, if you're not actively enjoying it, and if it takes up space you wish you could use for something else, it's time to do something about it.

This probably won't surprise you: I recommend keeping just a couple of the best pieces if you must and getting rid of the rest of the collection by selling it or giving it away.

But isn't there some kind of universal law that says you can never break up a collection?

As you'll recall, I broke up my collection of Nancy Drew novels. I didn't have the entire collection to begin with, but I had plenty, and I'd dragged them around for most of my life. My daughters read them and enjoyed them. Perhaps my granddaughters would also have enjoyed them some day (they can't read yet). But I didn't have room for my Nancy Drews anymore, and let's be honest: I was never going to sit down and read through all of them again. So I pulled out my three favorites and gave away the rest. Nothing bad happened; I was not struck down by lightning. I'm living proof that it's OK to break up a collection.

Sometimes it's easiest to shrink the collection over time. Years ago, my husband and I frequented estate sales and began bringing home old radios. These were beautiful large creations made of wood, not little transistor radios. Once polished, they were a sight to see, and we incorporated them into our decorating scheme. But as our family grew, our home seemed to shrink; playpens, riding toys and the like took over. It soon became obvious that we had too many radios. So we began giving them away, one at a time, over the years. Today we have just one big beautiful wooden radio, one of the first ones we ever bought. We love it, enjoy it and have no guilt over breaking up the collection.

Other times, it's best to get rid of the entire collection, or the majority of it, all at once. When we lived in our largest family home, we had a big kitchen without soffits, so three walls of cabinets had open space above them. I began collecting teapots that I found at estate sales to put up there. For years, my teapots lived in a long, tidy and colorful parade above my kitchen cabinets. Then we moved a few times before settling into our little house. Not only is there no open space above my kitchen cabinets now, there aren't even very many cabinets. So I found all my teapots among the moving boxes and looked at them as a group. I then began removing them, one by one, until I was left with my favorite three teapots to put on my china cabinet. The rest went straight to the Goodwill with no regrets. They served their purpose in my old kitchen, and weren't needed in my new one.

I didn't take photographs of the collections I've given up, but I wish I had, because they were fun to put together, and the process of doing so made for good memories. If you give up some or all of a collection, take a photo of it in its entirety first. You won't regret it, even if you're not really into those items anymore.

I gave away my old collections because I didn't have the time or desire to sell them. I probably could have made a few dollars off of them. If you decide to sell all or part of a collection, online or in a garage sale, be sure to include any names from your collection or even the title of the collection in your ads and on **craigslist.org**, where people can find it as a result of a search. That way people who collect what you did can find you and take things off of your hands for cash. For instance, if you're selling your paperback book collection, include the names of authors who are well-represented in it.

Some collectors are so passionate about their collections that they'll travel quite a distance to find and buy their next acquisition. When Eddie cleaned out his late father's apartment, he found a very old toaster that still worked. He posted it on **craigslist.org**, but no one in his area contacted him about it, and he soon forgot about the ad. A month later, he received inquiries about the toaster from two different states; he ended up selling the toaster to a man who would soon be flying to a city three hours away from Eddie on a business trip. The man ended up driving over six hours round-trip to snag Eddie's dad's old toaster, and he happily paid full price for it, saying it was exactly the model he needed for his collection.

The Truth about Collections

Whatever you collect, be honest with yourself about your actual desire for the items in each of your collections. Keep only what you need and love, and be fearless about breaking up collections whenever necessary. You have a desire to declutter your home and reduce your burden; don't sabotage yourself by letting the sentimental desire to keep a collection you no longer love or display gain the upper hand. You may have spent many years and many dollars collecting certain items, but consider that doing so gave you pleasure at the time; it's not a waste of money to give them to someone else who might like them now. If you sell the items at a consignment shop or on a specialty website, you may even get a few of those dollars back. (Remember, giving or selling something to someone who loves it greatly eases the pain of letting it go.)

If you have one or more collections that still bring you joy, enough that you keep them on display, consider rotating your collections. Put one out for a while and leave the others in storage, then regularly swap them out. My public library often displays a patron's collection for a month, so that others can enjoy it. The next month, they display someone's else's collection of something else. You can do the same thing in your own home with your own collections.

Once you realize that you have a tendency to collect things because you're sentimental, you'll need to keep control of current and future collections so they don't get out of hand. For instance, I love Kewpies, and I have three small Kewpie statuettes, but I would never collect them because I know me; if I let myself, I could amass an entire army of Kewpies in no time. I have no room for that in my home, so I just enjoy the three I have, one of which I was given as a child, and two that are recent gifts from my sister.

Some people believe that when you have a collection of anything, it's your job to keep it organized by inventorying it, taking and filing photos of all of it, keeping it clean and dusted, and storing or displaying it safely and securely so it won't come to harm. Whew! That sounds like too much work, and is an incentive for me to try *not* to collect things.

If reducing or giving up a collection still sounds too difficult to you, remind yourself that there are many beautiful collections in the world, but no one has the space to keep them all. Nevertheless, if you have an irresistible urge to create more collections, even though you don't have room for them, consider joining **Pinterest.com**. Collecting photos of things you love on Pinterest takes up no space, yet you get all of the fun of finding things (the thrill of the hunt) and adding them to your groups/boards.

Finally, if you tend to keep too many collections of too many things, and you suffer so much distress over giving up things that you fear you might be a hoarder, consider that there *is* a connection between collecting and hoarding. However, according to Dr. Susan Krauss Whitbourne in an article at **PsychologyToday.com**, while both collectors and hoarders can have trouble giving up items in their collections regardless of value, and feel great unhappiness at doing so, hoarders collect things in much larger numbers than mere collectors, and rarely display or show off their collections, which cause turmoil, shame and regret in their lives.

Items That Represent a Lost Dream

Ursula always intended to take her boys camping. Over the years she collected an impressive number of camping supplies that she found on clearance each fall while out shopping. But the busy single mom never found the time to actually go camping. Her boys were athletes, so their weekends and summers were always filled with practices and sports camps. (Later on, Ursula realized that fear of taking the boys camping by herself also came into play.)

Now her boys are grown and gone, but Ursula can't let go of the dusty but new-in-the-package tents, air mattresses and camp stove (with supplies). She's hoping maybe one of the boys will get married and have kids, and then she can take her grandchildren camping. But neither of her sons even has a steady girlfriend.

Ursula knows she should get rid of the camping equipment, but she's having trouble letting go of the dream it represents. Lately she's been thinking that it would be nice to keep her car in the garage once winter arrives. But there's no room for it because the camping equipment takes up so much space. Once she accepts the death of her family camping dream, she won't have to clean off her car on snowy winter mornings anymore.

Some people can look at things they bought that they never used, and pitch them or sell them without a second thought; that's the logical way to do things. The general idea is, if you never used it, why are you still tripping over it? But sentimental people have a much harder time doing that, because those items represent lost dreams, unfulfilled plans and sometimes even hope for the future:

- "As soon as things slow down at work, I'm going to take time off and finally update the kitchen" (with the paint and wallpaper border bought in 2002).

- "Someday I'm going to buy a cabin in the woods and become a writer" (surrounded by 10 years' worth of Amazon orders of how-to-be-a-writer books that have never been cracked open).

- "I've been collecting cute athletic wear in my goal size for years so I'll be ready when I finally get thin enough to start exercising in public" (after almost as many years of unsuccessful dieting attempts).

Some of these dreams are lost due to procrastination; others just never seemed to work out. In many cases, emotional issues are tied to items that represent a lost dream. It can be quite painful to admit to yourself that something you once wanted very badly (and maybe still want) not only didn't happen, but isn't ever going to happen. Giving up the items is a permanent step that forces you to acknowledge the death of your dream.

Ursula's sons are never going to be kids again. Even if she eventually has grandchildren, and she can take them camping, it won't bring back her sons in little-boy form. She had hopes invested in that camping equipment, but those hopes cannot become reality now.

Until we do the emotional work required to accept the loss of our dreams or our failure to achieve our ambitions, we'll just spin our wheels trying to get rid of things we bought but never used. Anytime we have great difficulty giving up something, we need to do some good, hard thinking about why we're having that trouble. Here are some lost dreams that I, and others, have struggled with.

The Freedom of Youth

Ginny and her husband Charles moved 17 times in 30 years, thanks to his career. Early on, she became an expert at distilling the sum total of their possessions down to a manageable level that made their many moves as painless as possible. But there was one box that she had never been able to give up: it contained the jacket, jodhpurs and boots she wore while taking weekly horseback-riding lessons, the summer she turned 14.

How she had loved that horse, Starbaby, and the times they shared together. Ginny had many fond memories of that summer, and they were still vivid even though she hadn't opened the box of clothes in years. But every time she moved, the familiar white and red apple box that held her treasures automatically went along.

When she was younger, she kept the clothes because she knew she'd need them once she started riding horses again. But the demands of her family and their frequent moves never left any time for horseback riding. Now, Ginny accepted that she had gotten taller (and heavier) since she was 14, and there was no way she could fit in those clothes. So what was the problem? Why couldn't she just let that box go? It almost felt as though it had some strange power over her. In retrospect, she realized, that's why she hadn't opened it for ages, and she was afraid to do so.

Charles was no help. He thought it was ridiculous that she still had the box. On the other hand, her best friend Tanya told her to keep the box since it meant so much to her. But Ginny was really bothered by the fact that she couldn't let it go.

The light bulb moment arrived after a phone conversation with her younger sister Lorraine. They were talking about their teen years.

"Oh, how I hated high school!" Lorraine sighed. "I couldn't wait to get out of there. It seemed like I was stuck there forever."

"Not me," Ginny replied. "I felt like it flew by."

"Well, sure, that's because you were Miss Perfect. Straight A's, in all the popular activities, cheerleader, lifeguarding in the summers....we hardly ever saw you once you got to high school," Lorraine said.

That night Ginny thought about her high school years. She was indeed very busy once she got there. In fact she'd been very busy ever since, what with college, marriage, children and all their moves. That summer before high school was the last time she'd felt truly free, cantering along the riding paths of the ranch where Starbaby lived, practicing what she'd been taught. With the breeze in her hair and the open acreage of the ranch all around her, she imagined that she and Starbaby were the only living creatures in the world, and it felt wonderful.

She hadn't felt truly free since then, she realized. There had always been too many things to do, too many demands on her time. But since their most recent move, she had yet to find a new job and was struggling with all the spare time she had now that her children were on their own. Maybe if she learned how to handle the first free time she'd had since she was 14, Ginny thought, she'd find the key to the emotions that were tied up in that apple box. Maybe she'd even be able to let it go.

The years of our childhood and young adulthood are hugely important in our personal histories. If you're having a hard time letting go of something from your youth that the logical part of your brain tells you to let go of, consider what it might actually represent to you. Take time to think hard about this. You might surprise yourself.

The Life You Planned On

We all make plans for our lives when we're young, but life doesn't always work out the way we planned. Often, we find new things to do, new people to do them with, and we grow in a different direction than we thought we would, back when we were young.

This is normal, but if, over the years, we collect items that we intend to use to someday fulfill those original plans, we can accumulate a lot of clutter, thanks to our good intentions. So if you have a collection of items that are part of a dream you once had (and maybe still have), don't just stuff those things back under your basement steps. Make a commitment to use them, or get rid of them.

Jason loved art when he was a boy; he always got A's in art class (and C's or worse in everything else). After high school, he intended to go to art school and become an artist, but his parents couldn't afford the tuition. Instead, he took a job as a plumber's apprentice so he could learn a trade to pay the bills. But he had a very clear picture in his head of living in a cottage near a lake up north and painting "en plein air," or in nature. He imagined selling his work at art shows and at galleries in the city. Realistically, he understood that it would be very hard to earn a living as an artist. So he figured he'd work in plumbing for a while to save up money.

Plumbing paid well. Over the years Jason bought a nice house and a few motorcycles that enabled him to travel the country with his brothers or some friends whenever he could take a vacation. Between work, keeping up the house and maintaining the bikes, there was little time to paint. But the thought of becoming an artist never left Jason's mind. He occasionally bought canvases, brushes and paints, and put the bags in the spare room, waiting for the day when he would finally be able to paint full time.

One September, Jason decided it was time to embark on his artistic plans. He turned down the chance to zip down to the Florida Keys with the guys in his bike club, and instead booked a lakeside cottage in Minnesota for two weeks. He packed one bag with clothes and another with paints, brushes and a few other things. He bought an easel and put it in his truck along with several blank canvases. Then he set off alone for Minnesota.

It was very quiet on the lake. In the cottage, Jason set up temporary housekeeping, and then arranged his easel and art supplies on the deck. This was it: the first step toward his new life as an artist. He decided to paint his view of the lake.

Painting was harder than it had been in his daydreams. What he put down on canvas didn't resemble what he pictured in his head. He knew he had artistic ability, but he wasn't sure how to tap into it anymore. Still, he kept plugging away.

After a few days, he had almost completed his first painting. But it didn't look like he wanted it to look. Soon, the quiet of the lake and the cottage began getting to him. He decided to have dinner at Dizzy's, a supper club he'd passed on the highway coming in.

He had a beer at Dizzy's bar, where he met a few other bikers and talked shop. Seeing he was alone, they invited him to eat with them. After a few more beers, some delicious fried walleye and the house salad, Jason was full and ready to retire, but not before making plans to meet his new friends again Friday at Dizzy's famous fish fry. The next day, he tried to paint for a few hours but quickly became frustrated. He realized that he was looking forward to the fish fry more than he had been looking forward to painting again.

Jason decided that he'd just forgotten how to paint freely, as he had when he was a kid. So he tried painting wild, crazy designs, rainbows, fireworks, anything that used lots of colors and might help him find his groove. He could see he was improving a little, but he still wasn't getting to where he wanted to be. But he kept at it until a few days before his two weeks were up, when he decided he'd had enough. He packed up and headed home.

It took a while to accept that the artist's life was not for him. But Jason, being nothing if not practical, soon faced the truth, boxed up his art supplies, and cleared out the spare room. It had been a nice idea, but he had clearly outgrown the dream.

What dreams have you outgrown? Take a look at your collected clutter. Were you going to become a master of Chinese cuisine? Build your dream house? Make your tap-dancing comeback as soon as you got back into shape?

Dreams are great, but reality is underrated. Be honest with yourself about your dreams and whether there's still a chance that you can achieve them. If you have hobby supplies that you always intended to use, make the time to try them again (or maybe for the first time). Do as Jason did and give it a real shot. You may find that the dreams are no longer what you want, and then you'll be able to give up the related clutter much more easily. Should you find that you love what you're doing, you'll have begun achieving your dream. In either case, you're doing something instead of just dreaming about it, and that's progress.

Other Unfulfilled Plans

After I became engaged, I went to my local bookstore and special-ordered a book about how to make your own wedding gown. As it turned out, I didn't have time to make my gown, so I bought one.

I was going to use the book when my sister got married a few years later, but I had a new baby so I didn't have time to make my sister a gown, either. But I saved the book for the day when my little daughter got married. I lugged that book around for years, until I finally forced myself to let it go when we downsized several years ago.

A few years after we moved, my youngest daughter got married; she found her dream gown, which would have been way too complicated for me to make. So had I kept the book, I wouldn't have used it...again. Then, two years later, my eldest daughter eloped. See, I did the right thing giving up that book!

But why was it so hard for me to do? Well, I've been sewing since I was a girl. First I made doll clothes, then clothes for myself and my sisters, and later on, clothes for my children. I now realize that when I bought that book, I thought making a wedding gown was the pinnacle of dressmaking, and I once dreamed of reaching that milestone.

Letting go of such things is an admission that you didn't achieve those dreams. This can be hard to take. That said, how depressing is it to have *dozens* of items that represent unfulfilled dreams? Admit to yourself that you chose to follow different dreams, and give up these items now, unless you're certain that you still intend to pursue those old dreams, and soon.

During our downsizing, a time when we got rid of *so* many sentimental items, I kept a few things that I promised myself I would use. One was a needlepoint pillow kit from the 1980s. I loved doing needlepoint years ago, but it was one of the hobbies I set aside once motherhood took over. After my kids were grown and gone, I committed to making that needlepoint pillow, and I did, just a few years ago. It now sits on a chair in our living room. It doesn't have the giant hunter-green country-style ruffle the pattern called for; instead I put very basic tan velvet piping around it. I had fun making it, but I had to commit to completing the project so I could justify having kept the kit all these years. That said, I got rid of many other projects and kits after finally admitting to myself that I would never complete them. Hopefully whoever bought them at the thrift store where I donated them enjoys making those things now.

Sometimes we keep things because we like *the idea* of doing something more than actually doing it. The writer's life or the artist's life sounds wonderful, and is often depicted that way in movies and television shows. But the reality is that writing or creating art successfully requires a lot of hard work. It's much easier to just dream about that life (while accumulating the necessary tools or instructional books and letting them pile up). The knowledge that we spent so much time and money gathering those items can make it harder to give up the idea, and possibly even make us feel guilty. Yes, it's definitely easier to just dream, isn't it? But that doesn't solve our clutter problem.

We tend to make excuses to ourselves about why we never used the things we bought; one of the main excuses is that we just didn't have the time. That may be true, but unless we have time now and will spend it using those items, we might as well admit that our good intentions didn't work out, and move along the supplies, books or whatever was necessary to our plan to someone who might actually use them. Be firm with yourself: adopt the motto "Use it or lose it." Remember, you wouldn't be reading this book if your accumulated clutter didn't bother you. Let go of the things you know you're never going to use, and be rewarded with more open space and a less burdened mind.

Perhaps you do participate in a hobby or other avocation, but you have a hard time finishing things because you're easily frustrated when something isn't turning out well, or it's just too hard, or you get bored. As a result, you're surrounded by half-finished wood creations, or partially made stained glass projects. Quilters have a term for this problem: UFO's (UnFinished Objects). Are there a lot of UFOs in your home, your basement, and your attic? The sad truth is that some projects just don't get finished. But you honed your skills working on them, so they did provide some value. Why not donate them where someone else can find them and complete them?

Accepting the Real You

When we hang onto things that would have been part of the life we wanted that didn't happen, we weigh ourselves down emotionally, and keep ourselves from accepting who we really are.

Janice bought a set of china years ago that she displayed in a lovely china cabinet. She dusted the dishes and glass shelves monthly, even though it was *not* her favorite duty. Finally one day, something in her rebelled, and she thought, "I'm sick of dusting this stuff! Why do I even have it all? I never use it."

This provoked a flashback of buying the china in hopes of having a family someday, which never happened. Then there came the consoling thought she had often reverted to: that she could use the dishes when she had friends over for dinner parties. But she and her friends traveled a lot and loved trying different restaurants; she'd never hosted or even been invited to a dinner party. That was something she only ever saw in old movies. All of a sudden, Janice felt silly. Why had she kept the china and the cabinet for so long? Why had she let it hold her and her feather duster hostage? It was a visual reminder of things she wanted and never got. Janice decided that she had to start seeing herself as the person she really was: an independent woman with great friends who loved travel and good restaurants...and had better uses for that wall than an overstuffed china cabinet.

It's funny how we use things to make ourselves feel like we're someone else. The sight gag of an elderly man with a comb-over driving a new sports car is a classic example of someone who can't admit who he is. The car makes him feel like he's young and virile again. But anyone with eyes can see the truth.

What things are you storing that make you feel like you're someone else, someone with the life you wanted but didn't get?

- Do you keep buying (and storing) dangly earrings and spiky high heels for the day you can party like a celebrity instead of working a register at a discount store?

- Do you have drawers full of never-used athletic wear, and workout equipment collecting dust, until you have the time to work out regularly and turn yourself into a champion bodybuilder?

- Is your average-size house overstuffed with furniture, pillows, lamps, wall art and window treatments in an effort to have a model home like you see on television?

Once you realize that you've been storing (and tripping over) an awful lot of things that you intended for your hopes and dreams that didn't happen, you need to ask yourself: do you really want to live your life surrounded by the physical evidence of all the lives you intended to live? Or would you rather live in the moment and surround yourself only with belongings that reflect who you are, right now? Imagine how much freer you would feel if you weren't dragging all those lost dreams around.

Let go of the physical evidence of your lost dreams. Then make a commitment to yourself to stop buying things for a fantasy life you wish you had, but never got. *We all have dreams, but buying the items we need for those dreams ahead of time is how we become surrounded by way too much stuff.* Only buy clothes you can (and will) wear *now*. Only buy furniture, housewares, craft supplies, and instructional books that you need and will use *now*. Live in the present, and you can live with more space, and less of "the stuff that dreams are made of."

That said, don't give up a dream that's still important to you. Yes, we all grow and change over time, and some of the dreams we had are no longer important to us, so we can let them go along with the clutter related to them. But not having all that old dream clutter can free you up to start working on a current dream. So if you still have a dream, why not get started on it now in a small way, one that you can afford financially and especially time-wise? Then see where it goes. Just don't stockpile things related to your dream ahead of time.

Mementos from Our Youth

In most cases, our parents saved at least some memorabilia from our childhood: our newborn hospital bracelet, curls trimmed off in toddlerhood, a note in childish scrawl from when we were 6. And at some point, perhaps when we left home or when they left this world, that memorabilia became ours.

People who aren't sentimental can easily dispose of such stuff, even though it documents their own beginnings. But the rest of us not only hang on to it, but add to it. We keep our favorite marbles, balls and jacks, baseball or Pokemon cards, scout badges, ticket stubs from great concerts, dried corsages from proms, report cards and class schedules, and many other youthful mementos that sentimental people like to hang on to.

Now they reside somewhere in our homes, probably not where we can see them, but we know we have them. And we've balked at getting rid of them, because they're the equivalent of a time capsule of our lives, and who throws away time capsules? Nobody. A time capsule is meant to be examined. For those who remember the time period it covers, it's great for bringing back memories. For those who are too young to remember that time period, it's a tangible history lesson.

If you have boxes of mementos from your youth that are important to you, you don't have to automatically get rid of them. Instead, curate them.

What is curating? It's what people who run museums do. They examine historic artifacts and choose only the best items, those that are the most representative of their time. When you go to a museum, you'll rarely see multiples or duplicates. Museums have limited space, so a museum curator wants a variety of items, the sum of which offers a distinct picture of how things used to be in a certain time period.

Most of what a museum curator chooses is put on display, not stored in the museum's basement. That's because the whole point of assembling a group of artifacts is for the enjoyment and education of visitors.

Likewise, your childhood mementos do you no good if they're buried in boxes in the back of your attic. In curating your memorabilia, you'll do just as we've done with other belongings discussed in this book.

First, pitch anything that's garbage. This includes old newspapers and magazines that you saved but can't remember why, matchbooks from restaurants you stopped at on vacations with your parents, cool rocks that you kept in your pockets when you were seven, and the paper hat and matching napkin from your third birthday party. There will probably be things (like the birthday hat and napkin) that meant more to your parents than they do to you. If your parents are still living, you don't have to tell them that you got rid of such things. Also, pitch anything that you can't believe you kept and don't care about anymore, and anything that falls under the category of "I don't even remember this."

Donating and selling are the next two steps of the decluttering process that we've used throughout this book, but I'm guessing there won't be all that much to donate because childhood memorabilia tends not to be useful to other people. Likewise, you may not find many items with monetary value among the artifacts of your youth. There are exceptions, of course. If you decide you can finally part with your G.I. Joe doll, er, figure (sorry, guys!), you might be able to sell it for decent money since some people do collect G.I. Joes (do some research on **eBay.com**, for starters). And you may have tiny jewelry from when you were young that has monetary value because it's silver or gold. But most of your childhood memorabilia is probably best measured in nostalgic value, not monetary value.

I don't usually advocate unloading your clutter on other people, but in this particular category of the Sentimental

Seven, I'm going to suggest giving some things to others. If you have special young relatives and friends to whom you would like to give something from your childhood, now is the time.

Let's suppose you have a lovely birthstone charm bracelet that you wore when you were a young girl, and you also have several little nieces or granddaughters, one of whom was born the same month as you were. Why not give her that bracelet now?

Maybe your grandfather gave you the key to his old car when you were little. How you loved that key! When you got a little older, you realized that it wasn't going to do you much good because no car came with it, but you kept it anyways because you loved your grandfather so much. Do you have a nephew or grandson that might like that key? One of your adult children might even appreciate the historic value of it and want it as a tangible part of the past.

If there's something you've often thought of giving to someone special in your family, and perhaps have already told them about, give it to them now. Don't wait just because you're still emotionally attached to it. As wealthy philanthropist Percy Ross used to say, "He who gives while he lives, knows where it goes."

Margo had the gold confirmation cross her parents gave her when she made her First Communion. She promised it to her beloved granddaughter Charlotte. After Margo died in a car accident, her son Adam went through her jewelry box, looking for a necklace to go with the dress he would have to take to the funeral director. He found her favorite purple beads, but also happened to see the little gold cross necklace. Knowing what gold is worth these days, he pocketed it and later sold it to a gold dealer. By the time his sister Beth and her family arrived in town for the wake, it was long gone. Later, when the family went through Margo's belongings, Beth couldn't find the cross necklace, and had to tell a disappointed Charlotte that she didn't know what happened to it. Adam said nothing.

As with other sentimental items, giving them to someone who truly loves them can ease the pain of letting go. While going through her things before moving to a new house, Leslie decided it was time to give up her beloved Crissy doll with the long, flowing (and now slightly frizzy) hair. She gave it to her niece Ainsley. Imagine Leslie's delight when her sister posted a photo on Facebook of Ainsley with a huge smile on her face as she hugged the doll, and the phrase, "Thanks, Aunt Les! I love you!" Now Leslie is glad she made that decision.

Once you've found items that you can let go of and give to someone who might like them, you're left with the rest of your mementos. Now is the time for ranking and prioritizing them so you can decide what you'll keep. Remember, you're curating: keeping only the items that are most representative of your youth.

Chances are you think you know which items you'll want to keep or give up before you even start going through everything. But you may be surprised to discover that certain everyday items will evoke a response in you that you never expected. It might be the key ring with the key to your first car, an old perfume bottle that holds only the faint scent of your favorite perfume when you were 20, or a pay stub from your first job. Include these items when you prioritize your sentimental things.

If you've kept your childhood diaries, reread them before deciding whether or not to keep them. I kept some of my teenage diaries until I was in my 50s; then I finally read them and decided they weren't worth keeping. (Had I wanted to keep them, I would have scanned them into my computer and saved them on a CD, because I now live in a small house, where storage space is at a premium.)

Letters don't take up much space. So if you have some that you absolutely can't give up, keep them where you can read them occasionally. If, over time, you find that you don't really feel like reading them after all, it may become easier for you to get rid of them. If the letters have historic value, or simply value to your family, consider scanning them and saving them. You can easily email them to extended family members who would like to read them.

You can also scan bulky old yearbooks; scan only the important pages and the inside back-and-front covers with the autographs (if you still remember the people who wrote them).

Don't forget to take photos of anything you're letting go of in order to preserve your memories, if you think you need help doing so. You can always put the photos you took in a digital scrapbook, using **Shutterfly.com** or **Snapfish.com**, so you can keep the memories without the clutter. You might include a brief paragraph explaining the story behind each photo in the book; such a book might become a keepsake for your children or heirs someday, too.

Get rid of duplicates wherever possible. For instance, don't keep the ticket stubs from every high school football game you attended. Save the one from the very best game you remember, or the one that's in the best physical shape, and get rid of the rest.

Remind yourself of your space limitations as you sort through your childhood mementos. You can't keep it all, so only keep the very best, most sentimental and most representative items.

Re-purposing Broken or Outdated Items

You may discover that some of the things you've kept are broken; maybe you already knew that but kept them anyways because of their sentimental value. It's easy to say you should just throw such things out now that you're decluttering, but sometimes they have monetary value as well as sentimental value.

For instance, I had a silver ring set with a star-sapphire that my husband gave me when we were dating. Over the years, the ring wore thin; one day, the back of it just snapped. I took it to a jewelry repair man, who said he couldn't fix it. But when I suggested turning the sapphire setting into a small pendant for a necklace, he quickly sketched up a drawing of how it would look. Two weeks later, I had a necklace that I now wear with joy.

Then there was Lynne, whose horror at learning that movers had dropped a box of her mother's china turned to joy when her friend Nancy used the broken pieces to make circular mosaic stones for Lynne's garden. Now, each time she walks around her new yard, she sees the familiar colors and pattern of her mom's dishes.

Consider the materials an item is made of before making a decision to re-purpose it. Obviously, sapphire, silver and china are worth reusing. But if your item is made of plastic (which dries out over time) or fabric (which rots), it may not be worth re-purposing. If the item was stored in extreme temperatures (in an unheated attic or storage unit), it may have sustained too much obvious damage already. In such cases, take a photo if you really want to remember the item, and then throw it away.

Smell is evocative; the problem is that most good smells don't last forever but are usually replaced by something less pleasant. Perfume turns rancid and ends up smelling like alcohol. Clothes with the scent of a loved one eventually start smelling musty. So if you keep something for the smell, accept that it won't stay that way. Once it turns, you'll have an easier time getting rid of it.

Certain clothes from our early years can be hard to give up. I married quite young, and vowed I would never give up my wedding gown. I kept it, along with the veil, all these years, hoping one of my daughters might wear it. Recently, one got married; my gown wasn't her style, so she bought her dream wedding gown. It was quite ornate, so she needed a simple veil to balance it out. I took my 1970s veil, cut off the chunky lace and the large headpiece, and made her veil out of what was left. She looked lovely in it.

Displaying Your Very Best Mementos

So you're left with your very best, most treasured mementos from your youth. Now what? Does it make any sense at all to pack them in boxes and put them back into storage? Those items are only worth keeping if you're actually going to look at them. Let's consider some ways that you can make them more accessible.

Hopefully, you were able to cull your personal time capsule down to a manageable size. Consider buying a decorative box with a lid, or a basket with a lid, to keep your mementos in. Then put it in a room where you can easily access it, so that you'll be more likely to go through it from time to time.

If you'd like others to be able to enjoy your mementos, put them on display in your home. For instance, you can keep small items in a large bowl, like a big fishbowl, or a large snifter (I've seen nice, large vintage snifters on **eBay.com**). This kind of display is ideal for:

- Scout pins and badges
- Honor roll or other lapel pins and buttons
- Charms
- Whistles
- Marbles
- Matchbooks
- School IDs
- Small toys and figures

Shadow boxes are a great way to display a group of different small items along with a photo or two; putting them under glass keeps them from getting dusty. You can use an old yearbook page or newspaper page for the background. Hang shadow boxes on the wall or stand them upright on a shelf or end table.

Speaking of end tables, a display end table is a useful piece of furniture that doubles as a conversation piece. Fill one with your precious mementos and you'll be able to see them all the time without having to dust them, thanks to the glass cover. Type the phrase "display end table" into a search engine and click "Images." You'll find display end tables in a variety of styles, some of which will surely blend with your decor.

If you've chosen to keep larger mementos, be sure you have room for them, and think about where you can display them, or keep them where you can get to them. As I said, I kept my wedding gown. It's in a large box in my storage area; it definitely takes up space, but I chose to get rid of many other things so that I could keep that box. It's not something I would display, however. But you may have a favorite teddy bear from childhood, or a framed picture that hung on your wall when you were growing up, that you just can't give up. Choose specific spots for such items and put them there.

Once you put your mementos from your youth on display, they will either give you joy every time you see them, or over time you'll get used to them, and at some point down the road, be able to let them go. Either one of those events is better than letting things molder away in storage.

Chapter 6 in a Nutshell

The Sentimental Seven can be particularly challenging to pare down, but the decluttering techniques in this section will help you reduce your sentimental clutter down to just your most precious things.

Chapter 7

Other People's Sentimental Clutter

I'm hoping that, after you read and absorb this book, you'll be very successful at decluttering and will end up with an uncluttered home, and more open space and available storage space than you ever dreamed possible. But if you don't live alone, you may not be able to obtain a *completely* uncluttered home because those you live with still keep too much stuff.

If they're not sentimental people, your impressive decluttering results will hopefully motivate them to clean up their own act. But if they're sentimental types, getting them to go through their own clutter will be a challenge, to say the least.

With any luck, the sight of your success will be the catalyst for their success. While (as you well know from your own experience) no one can *force* them to go through their own sentimental clutter, you can certainly encourage them. Here are a few tips:

• Offer to help, and follow through on your offer.

- If they don't want help, accept that they don't.

- Don't nag.

- Remember that this is a process; if they don't get rid of much at first, they may become more successful as they keep trying.

- Make them aware of people who need things they aren't using ("Hey, honey, the young couple next door are having a baby. Maybe they could use our old stroller, the one you kept even though our youngest is in junior high.")

- Accept that there's a middle ground between totally uncluttered and keeping everything.

- Remind them to take photos of anything they're nervous about getting rid of so they'll have that visual evidence if they fear losing the memories associated with it.

- Run interference by intercepting well-meaning nay-sayers who might derail them. (Example: when your significant other is successfully decluttering their closet, and their mother stops by; you *know* she'll say, "But there's still life in those old shirts!" if you don't keep her out of there.)

- Quote William Morris to them: "Have nothing in your house that you do not know to be useful, or believe to be beautiful."

- Emphasize how good it will feel to have more space in their room, or to see open space where there once were piles and stacks of stuff.

Finally, if you're trying to encourage one of your children to reduce their clutter, put a time limit on each decluttering session. They might work more quickly if they know there's an end in sight. I've also found that they'll be more motivated to go through their belongings right before their birthday and Christmas, once you remind them that they need to make room for the new goodies they're going to get.

———⟫◉⟪———

Chapter 7 in a Nutshell

Be encouraging and patient with other sentimental people in your household who need to reduce their excess belongings.

Chapter 8

A Final Word

Once you apply the principles I've shared in this book, you'll be on your way to being free of the burden of too much stuff that your sentimental self has been hanging on to for years, maybe for most of your life. It will be tremendously freeing to be rid of so many extra things you don't really need, while seeing and enjoying your truly special sentimental possessions whenever you wish.

Along with the information and advice I've given you, you'll need to maintain a positive attitude. Remember, you've *chosen* to reduce what you keep so you can live in a less cluttered environment. You've expressed a desire to live in a home where there are beautiful, meaningful items that warm your heart and bring back memories. (They'll be easy to see because they won't be surrounded by stacks, piles and boxes full of stuff.) The weight of far too many things will begin to lift as you let go of more and more possessions, and send them along to others who can benefit from them.

Decluttering can be a one-time event or it can be a process; the more sentimental you are, the more likely it is to be a process. Just try not to let it drag on too long or you'll give up in frustration, and the clutter will overtake you again.

The Second Time Around

Singer Frank Sinatra once had a hit song called "The Second Time Around." The first line is: "Love is lovelier, the second time around."

This may be true of love, but not of clutter. Clutter looks worse the second time around.

Nevertheless, you may find it easier to commit to regular rounds of decluttering instead of doing it all at once. This gives you time to reconsider keeping certain things, and will hopefully lead to your getting rid of things that you couldn't let go of before. Living in less clutter will help inspire you to do so.

When you declutter in stages, and you keep too much the first time through, later on you'll look at the items you kept and realize that most of them should have been moved along, too. However, some people (and you may be one), have a hard time getting rid of things on the second round simply because those things survived the first cut. So they begin second-guessing themselves. This is one reason why it's best to get rid of as much as you can the first time around. You probably won't even remember much of what you got rid of if you'll just let go of things during the initial round of decluttering.

However you choose to do this, remember to keep moving things along to their destinations by making regular trips to wherever you donate items to help others. Being diligent about doing this will produce results you can see, like emptier closets and dresser drawers with extra room in them. You'll be astonished at just how wonderfully motivating such sights can be.

Stay Motivated

If you do best when you have someone to help you, choose a friend or relative who will encourage you to keep going, and remind you of the reasons you're doing this. If you prefer to work alone, reread sections of this book that apply to the belongings you're going through; do so whenever you need more encouragement. It's easy to become overwhelmed by this task, so mentally prepare yourself for that feeling and do what you can to overcome it.

No Regrets

Occasionally I've missed one or two of the items I gave up when I decluttered. But I stopped feeling bad about that once I realized that if I hadn't gotten rid of those few things I missed, I'd still be tripping over the hundreds of things I gave away along with them.

It's natural to worry that you'll regret letting go of something you kept for years. But it's not the end of the world if it happens. At this point, ten years since our "big purge," I only regret giving up my kids' high chair, which I intended to use when my future grandchildren visited. Yet I doubt I would have liked having it take up precious storage space for years until I finally did become a grandmother. I also suspect that it wouldn't look too good by now, given that we bought it in the early 1980s. Ultimately, my regret over the high chair is particularly silly since we easily found a second-hand high chair that our grandchildren now use when they visit. Once they outgrow it, I'm sure my husband will have to tell me, "No, we are NOT keeping this for our future great-grandchildren!" because I'll probably get emotionally attached to this high chair, too.

What If You Can't Give *Any* of It Up?

In a way, I was fortunate. I *had* to give up a good portion of my sentimental clutter. We were moving into a much smaller house and there was simply no room for it. No one had to push me to get rid of my precious things, which made it easier, because that's something you have to decide for yourself. I just decided to greatly reduce my collections and sentimental things because it was obvious that there was no room for them in my new house, and I didn't want to trip over so much stuff in the future.

Perhaps you don't have a pressing need to reduce your sentimental clutter. It bothers you, but when you try to go through it, you can't find anything you're willing to let go of. If this is the case, you may just need more time. Wait a while and try again. I gave up things in my 50s that seemed essential to my mental well-being when I was in my 30s and 40s. It's amazing what time can do.

If you know you need to declutter an area, but just can't make yourself do it, you might have to wait until your desire for more space becomes greater than your desire to keep all of your sentimental items. After my youngest daughter moved out, I left her bedroom untouched for a few years. But once I decided to turn it into a sewing room, it was much easier for me to go through everything so that I could move my sewing machines and fabric stash in there.

Try this: make a note on your calendar for six months from now to reread this book (or Chapter 5 at a minimum), and then go through your boxes of sentimental things and collections again. When you do, be honest with yourself about anything that no longer seems to be a must-keep item; let go of it. Even if you only give up one piece of paper or a souvenir, that's progress. Do this every six months. I'm betting you'll give up more things as you go along.

And remember, you don't have to get rid of every single thing. Scattered throughout your collection of sentimental clutter is a nucleus of items, those that are most important to you, and you can find them and keep them. They'll be the few things that help you "touch" your late loved ones and even the person you used to be. They'll be shared with your children or your friends. They may even be the only connection between generations of your family. Find those few things, that nucleus, and you'll be able to give up the rest of your sentimental items much more easily.

⊰●⊱

This Book in a Nutshell

*In this book, I've described a way to declutter your home and reduce an excess of possessions without giving up your most precious belongings. Doing so is a process that takes time and is a lot of hard work. People who aren't sentimental can do it quickly, especially if the belongings aren't theirs; they just pitch everything. They have no concern for the value (historic or monetary) of family heirlooms, the items a loved one created or items representing childhood dreams or personal achievements. But those of us who are sentimental feel differently. So we have to accept that it may take longer for us to declutter, but that doing so carefully and with respect for the memories involved will make it worth our efforts, no matter how long it takes us. The end result will be more space and more freedom. We may even fall in love with our homes again, once we learn that we **can** declutter them, even though we're sentimental people.*

About the Author

Claire Middleton is a freelance writer who learned how to downsize and declutter after moving three times in four years, going from a 5-bedroom house to a tiny ranch, and selling or donating more than half of her family's possessions in the process. When she's not writing, she's usually in the kitchen or the garden.

Learn more about this subject and about Claire's other books at:

www.Claire-Middleton.com

Also by Claire Middleton

Downsizing Your Life for Freedom, Flexibility and Financial Peace

Attention, Baby Boomers and anyone else who is:

- Stuck in a rut and wishes for freedom…
- Unemployed and needs to move to a cheaper place…
- Overwhelmed and wants to simplify…
- …but has too much stuff to go through first.

In *Downsizing Your Life for Freedom, Flexibility and Financial Peace*, you'll learn about the joys of the downsized life:

- Lower personal expenses,
- Flexibility to move to wherever your career takes you,
- Clutter-free living, and
- More time to do what you love to do!

In *Downsizing Your Life for Freedom, Flexibility and Financial Peace*, Claire shares her story as well as those of others who learned the truth about possessions and freedom after downsizing their lives (voluntarily or not).

Learn more about this book at:

CardamomPublishers.com

SECRETS OF SMALL-HOUSE LIVING

Claire Middleton

Secrets of Small-House Living

The McMansion era is over! Today's home buyers are snapping up small houses while McMansions linger on the market. People are tired of caring for (and paying for) far more space than they really need, and they're learning that a small house is the answer to a financial reversal, an empty nest or simply a desire to live sustainably.

In *Secrets of Small-House Living*, Claire Middleton (author of *Downsizing Your Life for Freedom,*

Flexibility and Financial Peace) shows you how to take advantage of the small-house trend so you can have more free time to do what you enjoy…and more money left over at the end of each month.

In *Secrets of Small-House Living*, you'll discover:

- The advantages of living in a small house
- How to find the right small house for your needs
- How to choose which furnishings to take with you
- Decorating tips to make any small house feel comfy yet roomy
- Strategies for living well in a small house

If you're tired of the work and expense involved in living large, let *Secrets of Small-House Living* encourage you.

Learn more about this book at:

CardamomPublishers.com

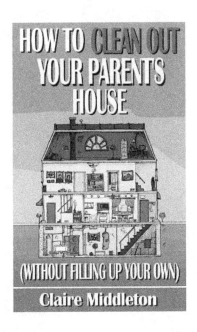

HOW TO CLEAN OUT YOUR PARENTS HOUSE

(WITHOUT FILLING UP YOUR OWN)

Claire Middleton

How to Clean Out Your Parent's House (Without Filling Up Your Own)

Going through your parent's estate is one of the hardest things you'll ever have to do.

Whether you're grieving a parent who recently passed away, or helping your increasingly frail parent liquidate their estate so they can move to a more appropriate environment (i.e. assisted living), you face the possibility of bringing roomfuls of your parent's belongings and family heirlooms into your own home. Where will you put these things? On the other hand, how can you bear to get rid of them?

The conflict created by those two questions lies at the heart of *How to Clean Out Your Parents' House (Without Filling Up Your Own)*. This book will help you honor your parent without keeping everything they owned.

Author Claire Middleton spells out the estate dispersal process for you, step by step, in this book. You'll learn:

- 14 methods for fairly dividing estates between family members

- what to keep for yourself

- how to organize the dispersal process (whether you're sole heir or one of many)

- secrets for sorting through the estate efficiently

- tips for determining the best destinations for valuables

As for those items that no one wants, find out how to move them along in a way that's respectful to your parent (or their memory).

Claire wants to help you avoid the mistake so many people make by moving all of their parent's belongings into their own attics, basements, closets and drawers, only to trip over them and work around them for years. Some never disperse their parent's estate, leaving it all for their own family to face after they die.

Surely you don't want to do that to your children! Use this book to go through your parent's estate promptly and efficiently so that their treasured possessions get good homes and their least important belongings don't end up in *your* home.

Learn more about this book at:

CardamomPublishers.com